Real-World STEM: Eliminate the Threat of Nuclear Terror

Other titles in the *Real-World STEM* series include:

Real-World STEM:
Eliminate the Threat
of Nuclear Terror

Bradley Steffens

San Diego, CA

© 2018 ReferencePoint Press, Inc.
Printed in the United States

For more information, contact:
ReferencePoint Press, Inc.
PO Box 27779
San Diego, CA 92198
www.ReferencePointPress.com

LIBRARY OF CONGRESS CATALOGING-IN-PUBLICATION DATA

Name: Steffens, Bradley, 1955–
Title: Real World STEM: Eliminate the Threat of Nuclear Terror/by Bradley Steffens.
Description: San Diego, CA: ReferencePoint Press, Inc., 2018. | Series:
  Real-World STEM | Audience: Grade 9 to 12. | Includes bibliographical
  references and index.
Identifiers: LCCN 2016056742 (print) | LCCN 2017006541 (ebook) | ISBN
  9781682822418 (hardback) | ISBN 9781682822425 (eBook)
Subjects: LCSH: Nuclear warfare—Prevention. | Terrorism—Prevention.
Classification: LCC U263 .S7244 2018 (print) | LCC U263 (ebook) | DDC
  363.325/56--dc23
LC record available at https://lccn.loc.gov/2016056742

CONTENTS

GREAT ENGINEERING ACHIEVEMENTS 6

INTRODUCTION 8
An Ominous Threat

CHAPTER 1 12
CURRENT STATUS: Blocking the Pathway to a Bomb

CHAPTER 2 27
PROBLEMS: Identifying Gaps in Security

CHAPTER 3 40
SOLUTIONS: Safeguarding or Eliminating
Nuclear Materials

CHAPTER 4 53
SOLUTIONS: Tracking, Detecting, and Stopping
the Use of Nuclear Materials

SOURCE NOTES 67

FIND OUT MORE 71

INDEX 73

PICTURE CREDITS 79

ABOUT THE AUTHOR 80

Great Engineering Achievements

 1 Electrification
Vast networks of electricity provide power for the developed world.

2 Automobile
Revolutionary manufacturing practices made cars more reliable and affordable, and the automobile became the world's major mode of transportation.

3 Airplane
Flying made the world accessible, spurring globalization on a grand scale.

4

Water Supply and Distribution
Engineered systems prevent the spread of disease, increasing life expectancy.

5 Electronics
First with vacuum tubes and later with transistors, electronic circuits underlie nearly all modern technologies.

6 Radio and Television
These two devices dramatically changed the way the world receives information and entertainment.

7

Agricultural Mechanization
Numerous agricultural innovations led to a vastly larger, safer, and less costly food supply.

8

Computers
Computers are now at the heart of countless operations and systems that impact people's lives.

9 **Telephone**
The telephone changed the way the world communicates personally and in business.

10 **Air Conditioning and Refrigeration**
Beyond providing convenience, these innovations extend the shelf life of food and medicines, protect electronics, and play an important role in health care delivery.

Highways

Forty-four thousand miles of US highways enable personal travel and the wide distribution of goods.

Spacecraft

Going to outer space vastly expanded humanity's horizons and resulted in the development of more than sixty thousand new products on Earth.

Internet

The Internet provides a global information and communications system of unparalleled access.

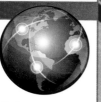

13

Imaging

Numerous imaging tools and technologies have revolutionized medical diagnostics.

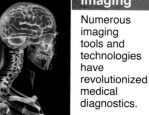

Household Appliances

These devices have eliminated many strenuous and laborious tasks.

Health Technologies

From artificial implants to the mass production of antibiotics, these technologies have led to vast health improvements.

16

Petroleum and Petrochemical Technologies

These technologies provided the fuel that energized the twentieth century.

Laser and Fiber Optics

Their applications are wide and varied, including almost simultaneous worldwide communications, noninvasive surgery, and point-of-sale scanners.

Nuclear Technologies

From splitting the atom came a new source of electric power.

High-Performance Materials

They are lighter, stronger, and more adaptable than ever before.

Source: Wm. A. Wulf, "Great Achievements and Grand Challenges," National Academy of Engineering, *The Bridge*, vol. 30, no. 3–4, Fall/Winter 2000. www.nae.edu/File.aspx?id=7327.

An Ominous Threat

"Nuclear terrorism is one of the most serious threats of our time."

—Ban Ki-moon, secretary-general of the United Nations

Ban Ki-moon, "Statement Attributable to the Spokesperson for the Secretary-General on the Entry into Force of the International Convention for the Suppression of Acts of Nuclear Terrorism," United Nations, June 13, 2007. www.un.org.

E ver since the United States dropped two nuclear bombs on Japan in 1945, killing more than one hundred thousand people, there have been warnings from world leaders, policy experts, scientists, and others about the dangers of a nuclear holocaust. For decades, concern centered on tensions between the United States and the Soviet Union as the most likely cause of a nuclear war. Although the United States and the Soviet Union came perilously close to using nuclear weapons during the Cuban Missile Crisis of 1962, neither they nor any nation armed with nuclear bombs have unleashed the devastating weapons since World War II.

There have been hundreds of armed conflicts since the end of World War II, leaving millions of soldiers and civilians dead. Several wars are ongoing, including the war in Afghanistan, Nigeria's Boko Haram insurgency, and the Syrian civil war. While nuclear weapons have not been employed in any of these conflicts, it is possible that nuclear bombs—especially small, tactical nuclear bombs—could be used in future wars. However, most security experts now believe the greatest threat to peace is presented by terrorist organizations—groups that attack civilians to further a political cause.

Terrorism on the Rise ■

According to the Global Terrorism Database, there have been 150,000 terrorist attacks since 1970, including more than 75,000 bombings. United Nations secretary-general Ban Ki-moon warned about the threat of nuclear terrorism in 2007, declaring, "Even one such attack could inflict mass casualties and create immense suffering and unwanted change in the world forever. This prospect should compel all of us to act to prevent such a catastrophe."[1]

Experts know that terrorists are seeking nuclear weapons. On February 23, 1998, Osama bin Laden, the leader of the al Qaeda terrorist network, issued a fatwa, or religious ruling, calling for Muslims to oppose the United States and its allies. It read, "In compliance with Allah's order, we issue the following fatwa to all Muslims: The ruling to kill the Americans and their allies—civilians and military—is an individual duty for every Muslim who can do it in any country in which it is possible to do it."[2] Later that year, Bin Laden told *Time* magazine reporter Rahimullah Yusufzai: "Acquiring [weapons of mass destruction] for the defense of Muslims is a religious duty."[3] Although Bin Laden is dead, his orders remain in effect for al Qaeda.

The Islamic State (IS), the largest terrorist group in the world today, shares al Qaeda's goals, but it has more followers and much more money than al Qaeda ever had. By seizing oil in Iraq and selling it, the IS has billions of dollars at its command. The group has shown the ability to manage and implement large-scale attacks requiring long-term planning. In 2015 photojournalist John Cantlie, a hostage of the IS who has served as a spokesperson for the group, described how the terrorist organization plans to use its money to procure a nuclear weapon: "The Islamic State has billions of dollars in the bank, so they call on their *wilāyah* [branch] in Pakistan to purchase a nuclear device through weapons dealers with links to corrupt officials in the region."[4]

Types of Nuclear Attacks ■

There are three types of nuclear and radiological terrorism: detonating a nuclear bomb that creates an enormous blast, shock wave, and fireball; using a radiological dispersal device, or dirty

bomb, to spread radioactive material through the air, creating panic and disruption; and sabotaging a nuclear facility to release deadly radioactive material into the atmosphere.

Use of a nuclear bomb would be the most devastating type of attack. In a 2003 report, nuclear terror experts Matthew Bunn, Anthony Wier, and John Holdren estimated that a 10-kiloton weapon (smaller than the bomb dropped on Hiroshima during World War II) detonated at Grand Central Station in Manhattan on a typical workday would kill five hundred thousand people and cause at least $1 trillion in economic damage. Experts believe such an attack would have devastating effects far beyond the site of the explosion. In 2005 United Nations (UN) secretary-general Kofi Annan told the International Summit on Democracy, Terrorism and Security that the economic effects of a nuclear attack would push "tens of millions of people into dire poverty," creating "a second death toll throughout the developing world."[5]

The effects of a dirty bomb would be far less serious than those of a nuclear bomb. The conventional explosives used to spread the radioactive material might kill some people, but they would not destroy a large portion of a city the way a nuclear bomb would. The major effects of a dirty bomb would be fear, chaos, and economic losses. People would have to be evacuated from whole sections of the targeted city, disrupting their lives. Many businesses would be forced to close or relocate, possibly triggering a financial crisis.

The effects of sabotage of a nuclear facility would depend on the scope of the attack. It would not be nearly as destructive as the detonation of a nuclear bomb, but it could be worse than a dirty bomb. If terrorists succeeded in having a power plant's nuclear fuel overheat and melt, the effects could last for decades and cost billions of dollars. Many years after the Fukushima Dai-ichi nuclear power plant in Japan was destroyed by a tsunami, cleanup efforts still have not reached the highly radioactive nuclear fuel rods, which overheated and melted. The radiation is so intense that it destroyed the wiring in robots that were built to remove the melted fuel, even though the machines were engineered to withstand the effects of radiation. Officials estimate it will take at least forty years to clean up the site.

Preventing nuclear terror is largely an intelligence operation, but it also is an engineering challenge. Increasingly, engineers are being enlisted to secure the radioactive materials needed to make nuclear weapons, to detect such materials as they move around the world, and to track and help stop the terrorists who are intent on using them.

CHAPTER 1

CURRENT STATUS: Blocking the Pathway to a Bomb

"Securing nuclear stockpiles is the single most important chokepoint blocking the terrorist pathway to the bomb."

—Matthew Bunn, Martin B. Malin, Nickolas Roth, and William H. Tobey, nuclear terrorism experts

Matthew Bunn et al., *Preventing Nuclear Terrorism: Continuous Improvement or Dangerous Decline?* Cambridge, MA: Belfer Center for Science and International Affairs, 2016, p. 1. http://belfercenter.ksg .harvard.edu.

To launch a nuclear attack, terrorists must have radioactive materials—either a finished nuclear weapon or the materials required to build one. Preventing terrorists from obtaining such materials is the surest way of preventing nuclear terrorism. "To make a nuclear bomb, a terrorist group would have to have separated plutonium or highly enriched uranium (HEU)—materials that do not occur in nature and are likely beyond the ability of terrorists to produce," write nuclear terrorism experts Matthew Bunn, Martin B. Malin, Nickolas Roth, and William H. Tobey. "Hence, if all the world's nuclear weapons and weapons-usable nuclear materials can be locked down and kept out of terrorist hands, terrorists can be prevented from ever getting a nuclear explosive."[6]

Kinds of Radioactive Materials ■

Some radioactive materials can be found in nature. The atoms in minerals, such as uranium, plutonium, and thorium, are highly unstable, meaning they break apart, or decay, more rapidly than other elements. As the atoms decay, they emit radiation, such as alpha particles, beta particles, gamma rays, and electrons. This process is known as radioactive decay.

Because of their radioactive properties, uranium and plutonium are fissile; that is, they can sustain a nuclear chain reaction, breaking apart, releasing tremendous amounts of energy, and causing other nearby atoms to break apart and release energy. This makes uranium and plutonium ideal for use as fuel in a nuclear reactor or as the explosive core of a nuclear weapon. However, these materials are not pure enough in their natural state for any practical use. Naturally occurring plutonium exists only in trace amounts within uranium ore—amounts too small for any industrial application. Uranium is plentiful, but it must be treated, or enriched, before it can be sustain a nuclear chain reaction. Enriched uranium can also be used to manufacture plutonium. Nearly all of the world's supply of plutonium is artificially produced from uranium in nuclear reactors.

Radioactive materials are dangerous to human health. The particles they give off can alter and destroy cells in the body, causing cancer and other conditions. Because enriched nuclear materials are highly toxic, governments around the world regulate their creation, ownership, and use. In the United States the Nuclear Regulatory Commission (NRC) oversees the building and maintenance of nuclear reactors. The agency issues licenses that permit the use of nuclear materials for various purposes, such as scientific research, medical imaging, and nuclear power generation. The NRC also monitors the disposal of nuclear waste. Other countries have similar agencies overseeing their own nuclear industries. The unauthorized production and use of HEU and plutonium is forbidden by law worldwide.

Since world governments control the production and use of nuclear material, they are the main instruments for stopping terrorists from obtaining the deadly materials. Many of the world's efforts to prevent nuclear terrorism are focused on improving the ability of various governments to better control nuclear materials within their borders. Such efforts require cooperation between governments that might not be friendly toward one another. International diplomacy is vital to controlling nuclear materials and preventing nuclear terrorism.

The Nuclear Fuel Cycle

The multistep process that makes it possible to generate electricity from nuclear power is called the nuclear fuel cycle. The cycle begins with the mining of uranium ore **(1)**. After processing that yields a concentrated substance and conversion to a more usable form, the uranium undergoes enrichment **(2)**. The enriched uranium is then sent to a fuel fabrication plant **(3)**. There it is pressed and baked and then formed into ceramic pellets and encased in metal tubes that form fuel rods. The fuel rods are transferred to the nuclear power plant, where they will be used to generate electricity **(4)**. What happens next depends on the country. In some countries, the spent fuel (or radioactive waste) is immediately sent to a storage facility **(5)** to await final disposal. This is known as an open or once-through fuel cycle. In other countries, the spent fuel will be reprocessed **(6)** and recycled as new fuel at the fabrication plant. When spent fuel is reprocessed it is known as a closed fuel cycle.

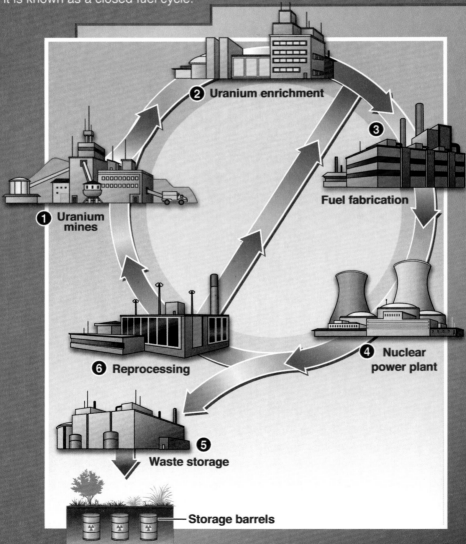

② Uranium enrichment

③ Fuel fabrication

① Uranium mines

⑥ Reprocessing

④ Nuclear power plant

⑤ Waste storage

Storage barrels

Source: European Nuclear Safety Regulators Group, "Nuclear Fuel Cycle." www.ensreg.eu.

International Agreements for Nuclear Security ■

After the discovery of the power of nuclear chain reactions, leaders from the United States and eleven other countries formed the International Atomic Energy Agency (IAEA), an organization that seeks to promote the peaceful use of nuclear material and to limit its use for any military purpose. Founded in 1957, the IAEA now has 168 member nations. The organization administers programs that outline international safeguards against the misuse of nuclear technology and nuclear materials. It created a clearinghouse for the transportation of nuclear materials from one country to another, so the whereabouts and amount of materials changing hands is known to regulators. Its Division of Nuclear Security plays an important role in helping countries around the world implement nuclear security measures. The agency offers recommendations and guidance on issues ranging from physical protection of nuclear materials to finding lost radioactive sources. The IAEA also created an incident and trafficking database so nations around the world are alerted to breaches in nuclear security.

The IAEA conducts physical reviews of nuclear security arrangements through an agency known as the International Physical Protection Advisory Service, or IPPAS. From 1996 through 2015 the IAEA organized sixty-nine IPPAS missions in forty-four countries. Forty-four of those missions involved nations that possessed separated plutonium or HEU, and sixteen were to countries that had operational nuclear power reactors but no weapons-grade nuclear material. The other nine countries that received visits did not have either weapons-grade nuclear material or an operating nuclear power plant but still needed knowledge and advice about nuclear waste, nuclear security, nuclear materials trafficking, and other issues.

To further strengthen the controls over nuclear materials, representatives of twenty countries met in Vienna, Austria, on October 26, 1979, and adopted an international agreement known as the Convention on the Physical Protection of Nuclear Material and Nuclear Facilities (CPPNMNF). "The Convention is the only international legally binding undertaking in the area of physical protection of nuclear material," states the IAEA, which holds the treaty and its instruments of ratification. "It establishes measures related to the prevention, detection and punishment of offenses relating to nuclear material."[7] The agreement provides for certain

Nuclear Terrorism Is Not Science Fiction

In 2005 UN secretary-general Kofi Annan spoke to the International Summit on Democracy, Terrorism and Security about preventing nuclear terrorism. In his speech he warns of real threats and mentions efforts being made by both the UN and by the Group of Eight (G8), an organization of eight highly industrialized nations that meets every year to discuss issues such as economic growth, crisis management, energy, and terrorism.

> Nuclear terrorism is still often treated as science fiction. I wish it were. But, unfortunately, we live in a world of excess hazardous materials and abundant technological know-how, in which some terrorists clearly state their intention to inflict catastrophic casualties. Were such an attack to occur, it would not only cause widespread death and destruction, but would stagger the world economy and thrust tens of millions of people into dire poverty. Given what we know of the relationship between poverty and infant mortality, any nuclear terrorist attack would have a second death toll throughout the developing world.
>
> That such an attack has not yet happened is not an excuse for complacency. Rather, it gives us a last chance to take effective preventive action.
>
> That means consolidating, securing, and, when possible, eliminating potentially hazardous materials, and implementing effective export controls. Both the G8 and the UN Security Council have taken important steps to do this, and to plug gaps in the non-proliferation regime. We need to make sure these measures are fully enforced, and that they reinforce each other.

Secretary-General Kofi Annan, "Keynote Address," International Summit on Democracy, Terrorism and Security, Madrid, Spain, October 3, 2005. www.un.org/News/Press/docs/2005/sgsm9757.doc.htm.

levels of physical protection during international transport of nuclear material. It also establishes a general framework for cooperation among states in the protection, recovery, and return of stolen nuclear material. One hundred fifty-three countries are now parties to the agreement.

Focusing on Nuclear Terrorism ■

While the IAEA and the CPPNMNF provide frameworks for controlling the spread of nuclear materials, they do not address terrorism specifically. Following the terrorist attacks on the World Trade Center and the Pentagon in 2001, US president George W. Bush and Russian Federation president Vladimir Putin launched the Global Initiative to Combat Nuclear Terrorism (GICNT). The GICNT is an international partnership designed to improve the ability of member nations to prevent, detect, and respond to a nuclear terrorist event. In the years that followed, eighty-six nations endorsed the GICNT Statement of Principles, which sets forth various nuclear security goals. GICNT member nations hold workshops, conferences, and exercises to share best practices for implementing the organization's statement of principles. Each year, the GICNT holds a meeting to discuss improvements and changes to the partnership.

US president Barack Obama also took steps to safeguard nuclear materials. In 2009 Obama told the UN Security Council:

> Although we averted a nuclear nightmare during the Cold War, we now face proliferation of a scope and complexity that demands new strategies and new approaches. Just one nuclear weapon exploded in a city—be it New York or Moscow, Tokyo or Beijing, London or Paris—could kill hundreds of thousands of people. And it would badly destabilize our security, our economies, and our very way of life.[8]

In 2011 Obama launched the Nuclear Security Summit as a way of strengthening international cooperation to prevent nuclear terrorism. The summits have focused the attention of dozens of presidents and prime ministers from around the world on nuclear security, often leading to action on issues that had been delayed or blocked. Because these summits focus on security, not disarmament or political issues, they have brought together representatives of nations that had never met on nuclear issues before. This includes leaders from nuclear weapon and non–nuclear weapon states, as well as states that have long-simmering animosities, such as Israel and several Arab nations and Pakistan and India.

The Nuclear Security Summits have discussed how to strengthen the nuclear security role of organizations such as the IAEA, UN, GICNT, and the international police organization, Interpol. At the 2014 Nuclear Security Summit, thirty-five countries signed an initiative to strengthen nuclear security, pledging to meet the objectives of IAEA security recommendations. The participating countries agreed to accept regular reviews of their nuclear security arrangements. In 2016 Jordan joined the nuclear security initiative, bringing the total of participating countries to thirty-six.

Securing Nuclear Weapons ■

The first and most important step toward eliminating nuclear terrorism is to make sure that all existing nuclear weapons are secured and accounted for. Although terrorists could build a nuclear weapon on their own, it most likely would not be nearly as powerful as the weapons already built and tested by the world's nuclear powers. Securing existing weapons has been the focus of many diplomatic efforts.

Currently, nine nations are known or believed to possess nuclear weapons: the United States, Russia, the United Kingdom, France, China, India, Pakistan, Israel, and North Korea. In addition, five more nations—Belgium, Germany, Italy, Netherlands, and Turkey—have American nuclear weapons stationed on their soil as part of a military partnership known as the North Atlantic Treaty Organization. The weapons in these five countries are under the control of the US military. Nuclear weapons have a central place in the defense of each country. As a result, each nation shrouds its weapons programs in secrecy and safeguards its own stockpile of nuclear weapons.

In spite of the extreme secrecy surrounding nuclear weapons programs, international diplomacy has succeeded in limiting the growth, or proliferation, of nuclear weapons. Some of these agreements are bilateral; that is, they are between two nations. For example, the United States and the Soviet Union agreed in 1972 to strictly limit the number of missiles that could be used to stop incoming nuclear weapons. Both sides believed that a buildup of such defensive weapons, known as antiballistic missiles, would be extremely costly. They also shared the view that a buildup would increase the likelihood of a nuclear war, since one nation, believing it had enough defensive missiles to protect itself, might decide to attack the other. The Treaty on the Limitation of Anti-Ballistic Missile Systems was the first agreement between the United States and the Soviet Union that placed limits and restraints on their nuclear weapons systems. Other bilateral agreements between the United States and the Soviet Union (now the Russian Federation) have followed. In addition, several multinational agreements involving several countries have been signed. For example, in 2009 the African Nuclear-Weapon-Free Zone Treaty went into effect. Under that treaty, thirty-nine African nations agreed not to develop, manufacture, acquire, or possess any nuclear explosive device.

Countries with nuclear weapons that are a party to the GICNT have stepped up the security of their weapons by participating in field exercises, workshops, and other activities. Even countries that have not signed the agreement, such as Pakistan, have taken steps to secure their nuclear arsenals. For example, Pakistani finance minister Ishaq Dar declared that a "special security force of 25,000 personnel, who have been specially trained and provided sophisticated weapons, has been deployed to protect [the nuclear assets]."[9] Pakistani officials also report that the country's weapons sites have been equipped with extensive intrusion barriers and detection systems and that the components of nuclear weapons are stored separately. "I'm convinced that Pakistan's nuclear weapons won't be allowed to fall into the hands of the insurgents," wrote US Department of Defense official Lawrence J. Korb after visiting Pakistan in 2009. "Given the strategic location of Pakistan and the fact that it has nuclear weapons, it's easy to see why some might embrace a worst-case scenario. But based on my visit, I don't buy it at this time."[10]

Protecting Weapons-Grade Nuclear Materials ■

Keeping nuclear weapons out of the hands of terrorists is a global priority, but the task is made simpler by the relatively small number of such weapons and the fact that they are under military control. The next highest priority is to prevent terrorists from obtaining the nuclear materials needed to build a weapon of their own—HEU and plutonium. This task is complicated by the fact that these materials are scattered all over the globe, not only in military installations, but also in nuclear power plants, research laboratories, and nuclear waste disposal sites. Nevertheless, progress has been made to secure such materials through the IAEA, GICNT, and other organizations. For example, thirty of the fifty-seven countries that once possessed weapons-usable nuclear material have eliminated it, in nearly all cases with help from the United States. This includes former members of the Soviet Union, such as Uzbekistan, Kazakhstan, and Georgia. In addition, security procedures have been tightened in every country where weapons-grade nuclear materials continue to exist.

The United States and Russia, the two countries with the largest amounts of weapons-grade nuclear material, have cooperated extensively to secure nuclear materials. In the past decade, engineering and security experts from the United States helped Russian security forces upgrade security at ninety-seven sites where nuclear weapons are stored. Together the Americans and Russians improved security at 218 of 229 buildings and bunkers that contain weapons-usable nuclear material. In addition, American and Russian engineers installed real-time surveillance systems in American and Russian nuclear disposal sites to ensure that there is no unauthorized access to storage containers of weapons-usable materials. "It is significantly more difficult to steal weapons-usable nuclear material in Russia than it was 20 years ago,"[11] state Bunn, Malin, Roth, and Tobey.

Progress also has been made in research laboratories that use HEU for scientific experimentation. Since 1978, 100 research reactors fueled with HEU have shut down. Another 65 have converted from HEU to low-enriched uranium. These changes are important, because research laboratories typically are not as secure as military facilities. The elimination of weapons-grade materials from 165 research sites has made it much more difficult for terrorists to obtain the materials needed to build a nuclear weapon.

Protecting Nuclear Power Plants ■

The nuclear materials used as fuel in nuclear power plants is not as pure as weapons-grade material. Weapons-grade uranium consists of 90 percent uranium 235. The fuel used in a nuclear

Two Kinds of Nuclear Bombs

Terrorists seeking to build a nuclear bomb have a choice of technologies to pursue: fission bombs and thermonuclear bombs.

Fission bombs, sometimes called atomic bombs or A-bombs, use a process known as nuclear fission to release large amounts of destructive force. Nuclear fission occurs when the nucleus of a heavy atom, such as uranium, is split into two lighter nuclei. To split the atom, nuclear engineers design a bomb containing both conventional explosives, such as TNT, and HEU. The force of the TNT explosion is directed toward the uranium atoms, causing them to split. This process releases a tremendous amount of energy that causes a chain reaction of more splitting atoms, which generates heat, radiation, and a tremendous shock wave.

Thermonuclear bombs, also known as hydrogen bombs or H-bombs, use a process known as fusion to generate even more destructive force than is possible through fission. Nuclear fusion occurs when the nuclei of two light atoms, such as hydrogen atoms, combine. Fusing two atoms releases even more energy than splitting one atom does. However, it takes more force to cause two atoms to fuse than it does to split an atom. In fact, conventional explosives do not create enough force to cause nuclear fusion. A fission reaction is required to trigger fusion. As a result, thermonuclear bombs employ both reactions: a fission reaction first, which in turn causes the even more powerful fusion reaction.

power plant is only 3 percent to 5 percent uranium 235, far below the level needed to build a bomb. However, the "burning" of nuclear fuel in some power plants creates plutonium as a by-product. The plutonium produced by nuclear power plants is mixed with other materials in the nuclear waste. The waste must be specially treated to separate the plutonium from the other materials. Currently, nuclear facilities in some countries, such as India and Pakistan, use a "closed" fuel cycle in which the waste is reprocessed and the plutonium is separated for reuse. Such plants can be a source of plutonium needed by terrorists to build a bomb.

Although nuclear power plant fuel is not pure enough to make a conventional weapon, it nevertheless is highly radioactive and dangerous to human beings. Terrorists could pack conventional explosives, such as TNT, around a core of uranium fuel or re-covered plutonium to make a "dirty bomb." Such a bomb would spread the radioactive material through the air, endangering any-one who comes in contact with it. Similarly, an attack on a nuclear power plant could release overheated nuclear fuel into the air, endangering those nearby. "If a 'dirty bomb' is detonated in a major city, or sabotage occurs at a nuclear facility, the conse-quences could be devastating," Yukiya Amano, director general of the IAEA, told the International Conference on Nuclear Security in 2013. "The threat of nuclear terrorism is real, and the global nuclear security system needs to be strengthened in order to counter that threat."[12]

Securing the nuclear material used by the world's nuclear pow-er facilities is a much larger task than securing its nuclear weapons. Thirty-one nations operate a total of 446 nuclear power plants, which produce about 11 percent of the world's electric power. Se-curity for these facilities typically is overseen by agencies of the various governments where they are located. The countries with the largest number of nuclear power plants—including the United States, Russia, the United Kingdom, France, China, India, Paki-stan, and Japan—are cooperating with the IAEA to improve nucle-ar security. The efforts include sharing best practices, sponsoring technical exchange visits to nuclear facilities, and conducting research on how to improve nuclear security.

In the United States the NRC, part of the US Department of Energy (DOE), regulates spent fuel through a combination of licens-ing, safety oversight, and regulatory support activities. In 1978 the DOE began to study several locations to permanently store used uranium fuel from the nation's ninety-nine nuclear power plants. After extensive study, the DOE recommended building a storage facility deep in volca-nic rock beneath Yucca Mountain in Nevada. In 2002 Congress passed and President Bush signed legislation designating Yucca Mountain as the nation's nuclear repository. However, concerns

A tunnel-boring machine begins drilling holes into a Yucca Mountain site to create a repository for America's nuclear waste. The project was started in 2002 by President George W. Bush, but in 2010 President Barack Obama halted the work due to long-term environmental concerns.

about the long-term environmental impact of the plan led Obama to halt funding for the project. According to the National Research Council, more than forty-two thousand metric tons of spent fuel are stored underwater in large spent-fuel storage pools for cooling and shielding purposes in the United States. Another three thousand metric tons of spent fuel are stored outside the power plants in dry casks on concrete pads. All of the spent fuel remains at the nuclear power facilities where it was produced.

Engineering Solutions in Use Today ■

Many engineering solutions have been deployed to prevent unauthorized people from gaining access to nuclear weapons, weapons-grade materials, nuclear fuel, and nuclear waste. Nuclear weapons facilities and nuclear power plants are surrounded by physical barriers such as fences and walls. The perimeters of the facilities are protected with camera surveillance and electronic sensors. Entrance to nuclear facilities is limited to a small number of people, who must present various forms of identification. Workers and visitors to many nuclear installations must undergo biometric identification such as fingerprint or iris scanning.

Additional safeguards protect stockpiles of nuclear weapons. The weapons normally are located deep underground so they cannot be destroyed by incoming missiles, bombs, or planes. Personnel with access to nuclear weapons must undergo thorough background checks and psychological testing to make sure they are not suffering from mental illness or harboring grievances that might cause them to act unpredictably and deploy a weapon. In many cases the nuclear warhead is not attached to the delivery system, such as a bomb or missile, so it cannot be launched accidentally. The warhead is stored near the delivery system to be attached when needed. In cases where delivery systems are armed, they cannot be deployed without receiving highly secret electronic arming commands known as a permissive action link. These commands cannot be given by one person. Using a human engineering principle known as the two-person rule, two secret codes—each known only to a separate individual—are required to arm the weapon. This safeguard makes it almost impossible for one person to launch a nuclear attack. Even an order from the president, who is the only person in the United States who can give the order to use nuclear weapons, must be confirmed by the secretary of defense.

> **WORDS IN CONTEXT**
>
> **biometric**
>
> identification of individuals based on the analysis or measurement of unique physical characteristics

Nuclear Detection at the Borders ■

Security measures have so far prevented the theft or capture of a nuclear weapon, but some weapons-grade nuclear material has gone missing. The IAEA's Incident and Trafficking Database has recorded eighteen incidents involving the attempted smuggling or sale of HEU or plutonium. In addition, the database notes 1,248 incidents reported by ninety-nine countries over the past twelve years that involve fuel-grade nuclear materials.

A radiation portal monitor in Buffalo, New York, scans passing trucks for evidence of nuclear material. Since the 2001 terrorist attacks, these devices have served as a part of America's line of defense against the unsafe or illegal transport of radioactive containers or devices.

To protect against this material entering the United States, the US Department of Homeland Security has deployed engineering solutions at border checkpoints and ports of entry. These measures are designed to detect radioactive materials entering the country. The radiation portal monitor (RPM) provides a nonintrusive, or passive, means to screen trucks and other vehicles for the presence of nuclear and radiological materials. The RPM system is similar to a radio receiver: It responds to certain types of energy emitted by radioactive materials, indicating the strength of the energy received. An RPM can detect radiation emanating from nuclear bombs, dirty bombs, enriched nuclear material, natural sources, and radioactive material commonly used in medicine and industry. More than fourteen hundred RPMs are deployed at US borders and a similar number at foreign locations for the purpose of intercepting illicit radiological and nuclear material.

Through international agreements, new and advanced technology, and an awareness of terrorist plots and ambitions, the security of nuclear materials has improved greatly over the years. Nevertheless, the growing use of radioactive materials in weaponry, power generation, research, and medicine means that even better engineering solutions will be needed to protect against nuclear terrorism in the future.

CHAPTER 2

PROBLEMS: Identifying Gaps in Security

"To date, the global nuclear security framework remains a patchwork, and does not include any agreed standards that specify what levels of security are needed for nuclear weapons and weapons-usable nuclear materials."

—Matthew Bunn, Martin B. Malin, Nickolas Roth, and William H. Tobey, nuclear security experts with the Harvard University Kennedy School of Government

Matthew Bunn et al., *Preventing Nuclear Terrorism: Continuous Improvement or Dangerous Decline?* Cambridge, MA: Belfer Center for Science and International Affairs, 2016, p. iv. http://belfercenter.ksg.harvard.edu.

Global efforts to eliminate nuclear terrorism are focused on keeping nuclear weapons and weapons-grade nuclear material out of the hands of terrorists. These efforts include cooperation between countries to tighten security through organizations such as the IAEA, GICNT, and the Nuclear Security Summit. They also involve the use of technological measures such as electronic surveillance of weapons sites, nuclear power plants, and nuclear research facilities. In addition, many countries have deployed high-tech systems at border checkpoints to detect the presence of radioactive materials and prevent illegal trafficking in the dangerous materials. Progress has been made in all of these areas. However, gaps remain. International cooperation on nuclear security is breaking down in some areas. The installation of radiation detection systems has stopped in several countries. Security systems have been breached both at weapons sites and inside nuclear power plants. Terrorists have infiltrated the military in some countries and performed sabotage in others. The countries that are most quickly expanding their nuclear arsenals and power plants are also among the most corrupt nations in the world, raising the possibility that nuclear weapons or materials might be sold to the highest bidder.

A Breakdown on Nuclear Cooperation ■

The most serious setback to eliminating nuclear terror has been the breakdown in cooperation between the United States and Russia. Prior to 2014 the United States and Russia were cooperating on a vigorous program to increase nuclear security. The United States was spending about $100 million a year to help Russia upgrade its nuclear security along its borders and at sites containing weapons-usable nuclear material. American security experts were actively supporting their Russian counterparts, and vice versa. Both countries were allowing real-time surveillance of their nuclear disposal sites so experts in the other country could verify they were secure.

These activities came to a halt in 2014. After protesters ousted the government of Ukrainian president Viktor Yanukovych in February 2014, Russian troops crossed the Russia-Ukraine border and took control of areas within Ukraine, including Crimea. On March 2, US secretary of state John Kerry called the Russian action an "incredible act of aggression" and "an invasion"[13] of Ukraine. Over the next three weeks, Barack Obama signed two executive orders authorizing sanctions against Russian individuals involved in the Ukrainian incursion. Russia retaliated by imposing sanctions of its own. In addition, Russia withdrew from the Nuclear Security Summit that Obama had founded in 2010. In response, the Obama administration cut off funding to upgrade nuclear security in Russia.

Security Gaps in Russia ■

With the loss of $100 million a year in financial assistance from the United States, the Russian program to upgrade the country's nuclear security came to a halt. Security overhauls at eleven Russian facilities that stored weapons-grade nuclear material were not completed. "The United States protects its nuclear weapons with barriers, guards, surveillance cameras, motion sensors, and background checks on personnel," writes the Council on Foreign Relations. "Russia's security measures are flimsier. Guards at nuclear weapons facilities have gone unpaid for months at a time, and even basic security arrangements such as fences, doors, and padlocks remain inadequate in many locations."[14] The installation of radiation detection equipment at Russia's bor-

The radioactive materials storage plant in Zheleznogorsk, Russia, was an important part of early Soviet nuclear weapons development. Since the collapse of the Soviet Union, experts worry such sites are not adequately protected against terrorists or other security threats.

ders has stopped, leaving a large hole in Russia's nuclear detection perimeter. The conversion of research reactors from HEU to low-enriched fuel also has stalled. "Roughly half of the world's remaining HEU-fueled research reactors are in Russia, which is no longer participating in U.S.-funded conversion efforts," write Bunn, Malin, Roth, and Tobey. "There have been dramatic delays in developing high-density fuels to convert research reactors from HEU fuel to less dangerous low-enriched uranium, and conversion efforts have slowed."[15]

The cut in funding for Russian nuclear security is of particular concern for two reasons. First, Russian nuclear officials are notoriously corrupt and might accept bribes in return for access to nuclear weapons or material. Second, the number of terrorists in Russia is growing. According to Transparency International,

A Hotbed of Uranium Smuggling

According to the IAEA's Incident and Trafficking Database, the smuggling of HEU or plutonium has been stopped eighteen times. Four of these incidents occurred in Moldova, a small eastern European country best known for its vineyards and wine. In each case the smugglers were planning to sell the material to terrorists. Three of the attempted sales were sting operations designed to break up the smuggling rings, but the fourth investigation uncovered an attempt to sell the nuclear material to an actual buyer from the Middle East.

In one case the smuggler sold the Moldovan investigators a section of a depleted uranium cylinder, possibly from the destroyed Chernobyl reactor. In another case the smuggler exchanged 200 grams of unenriched uranium for about $15,000. In a third case the smuggler sold a 10-gram sample of weapons-grade uranium for 320,000 euros ($360,000). The seller claimed to have 10 kilograms of HEU and blueprints for making a dirty bomb. The smuggler of the HEU repeatedly expressed hatred for the United States. "He said multiple times that this substance must have a real buyer from the Islamic states to make a dirty bomb," Constantin Malic, one of the Moldovan investigators, told the Associated Press. "He said: 'I really want an Islamic buyer because they will bomb the Americans.'" All of the smugglers were convicted of their crimes; however, the suppliers of the illicit materials were never caught.

Quoted in Associated Press, "Nuclear Smugglers Shopped Radioactive Material to Islamic State, Other Terrorists: AP report," *Chicago Tribune*, October 6, 2015. www.chicagotribune.com.

a global nongovernmental organization based in Berlin, Germany, Russia is one of the most corrupt countries in the world. In its 2015 report, Transparency International ranked Russia as the fifty-sixth most corrupt nation in the world, making it more corrupt than 119 other countries. This culture of corruption has already been seen in Russia's nuclear industry. In 2010 Major General Victor Gaidukov, the commander of a nuclear weapons storage facility, was relieved of his command amid charges that he stole US funds intended to be spent on nuclear safety and security. In addition, the director and two deputy directors of the Siberian Chemical Combine, one of Russia's largest HEU and plutonium processing facilities, were arrested in 2012 for accepting millions of dollars in bribes. More than $2 million in cash and three kilograms of gold bars worth more than $100,000 were found in the director's home.

Terrorists are aware of the Russian corruption. In an interview with Pakistani journalist Hamid Mir in 2001, Ayman al-Zawahiri, then al Qaeda's second in command and now its leader, stated, "If you have $30 million, go to the black market . . . , contact any disgruntled Soviet scientist, and . . . dozens of smart briefcase bombs are available."[16] Weapons-grade nuclear material is also available. In 2006 security forces in Georgia arrested a small-time smuggler named Oleg Vladimirovich Khintsagov, who had crossed the border from Russia to sell a small amount of weapons-grade uranium to a person he thought was a terrorist arms dealer, but who was actually a Georgian security officer taking part in a sting operation. Fearful of reprisals, Khintsagov refused to reveal the source of his uranium, but Georgian investigators believe he bribed Russian nuclear officials to obtain it.

The cutback in US security aid coincides with a growing terrorist threat within Russia. According to Russian president Vladimir Putin, five thousand to seven thousand Russians and citizens of other former members of the Soviet Union are fighting for the IS. Alexey Malashenko and Alexey Starostin of the Carnegie Moscow Center report that some of these Islamic extremists have moved into the Ural Federal District, where some of Russia's largest nuclear weapons–related facilities are located. The end of security funding from the United States has left Russian nuclear sites vulnerable to terrorist attack.

Deteriorating Global Cooperation ■

Russia's withdrawal from the Nuclear Security Summit has had far-reaching effects. The summit decided its 2016 meeting would be its last, dealing a blow to continued nuclear security cooperation. The number of nations participating in the organization's security initiative has stalled at thirty-six. Several countries with large stockpiles of weapons-usable nuclear material never signed the agreement. The nonparticipating countries include not only Russia, but also Pakistan, India, and China.

The deteriorating international cooperation has led the United States to reduce funding for nuclear security not only in Russia, but also in other countries. While the United States reduced security funding to Russia by $100 million, it also cut funding for other countries by $200 million. According to the Harvard Kennedy School, the United States is now spending less on its International Security Program than it has at any time since the 1990s. The Obama administration recommended further cuts in the future. "Current projections call for spending substantially less on nuclear security every year for the next five years than the government was projecting only one year ago," wrote analysts for the Harvard Kennedy School in 2016. "These spending reductions, if approved by Congress, would further slow nuclear security progress."[17]

Security Problems in Pakistan ■

The cutbacks in American spending are affecting nuclear security around the world. The impact on Pakistan is particularly worrisome, since that central Asian country is building nuclear weapons at a faster rate than any nation in the world. The weapons are housed in a growing number of locations, increasing the demands for security. Pakistan now has four nuclear reactors capable of producing weapons-grade plutonium. In addition, a plutonium reprocessing plant for handling the spent fuel from these reactors became operational in 2015. At the same time, Pakistan is a focal point of Islamic terrorism. "When you map W.M.D. [weapons of mass destruction] and terrorism, all roads intersect in Pakistan,"[18] Graham Allison, a Harvard professor and a leading nuclear expert, told the New York Times.

Established by its constitution as an Islamic republic, Pakistan is home to more than 200 million Muslims. It is the only Muslim nation to have declared that it possesses nuclear weapons. Many of Pakistan's citizens support Islamic extremist groups such as al Qaeda, the Taliban, Lashkar-e-Taiba, Jaish-e-Mohammed, and the IS. Some of these terrorist sympathizers are officials within the Pakistani government. One of the most prominent al Qaeda sympathizers is Sultan Bashiruddin Mahmood, a government engineer who helped design the nuclear reactor at Khushab that produced fuel for Pakistan's nuclear bomb. Mahmood told his associates that he believed Pakistan's nuclear bomb was "the property of a whole Ummah," or worldwide Muslim community. Mahmood said he wanted to share the nuclear weapon with those who might bring about "the end of days,"[19] leading the way for Islam to become the dominant force in the world.

When Pakistani officials learned of Mahmood's desire to share nuclear weapons with terrorists, they removed Mahmood from his position in the government. In August 2001 Mahmood traveled to Afghanistan, where he met with al Qaeda leaders Osama bin Laden and Ayman al-Zawahiri to discuss nuclear terrorism. "This guy was our ultimate nightmare," an American intelligence official told *New York Times* reporter David E. Sanger in late 2001. "He had access to the entire Pakistani program. He knew what he was doing. And he was completely out of his mind."[20]

Although Mahmood is no longer involved with the Pakistani nuclear program, other terrorist sympathizers remain within the government and military. In September 2014 a group of Pakistani naval officers recruited by al Qaeda tried to seize a Pakistani naval vessel. The plan was to use the vessel's nonnuclear antiship missiles to attack US naval vessels and provoke a firefight. The plot failed, but the Pakistani government admitted that the terrorists could not have staged the attack without help from terrorist sympathizers on the inside. "Repeated terrorist attacks on heavily guarded facilities in Pakistan—often appearing to have insider help—highlight the ongoing risk,"[21] write Bunn, Malin, Roth, and Tobey.

Like Russia, Pakistan has widespread corruption. Transparency International ranked Pakistan as the forty-ninth most corrupt country in the world, more corrupt than 126 other countries. The presence of a greater number of corrupt officials gives terrorist organizations more opportunities to use their funds to purchase secret information or nuclear materials for use in weapons. The case of Abdul Qadeer Khan, the founder of Pakistan's nuclear bomb program, demonstrates the danger corruption poses to nuclear security. In 2004 Khan confessed to selling Pakistan's nuclear secrets and materials to Iran, North Korea, and Libya. Khan also produced documents showing he was not the only one accepting bribes. According to his records, he gave more than $3 million to senior officers in the Pakistani military to gain their approval for selling secrets and equipment to North Korean scientists interested in building nuclear weapons.

Security Breakdowns in India ■

Cutbacks in American nuclear funding have also affected India. So far, nuclear security cooperation between the United States and India has been limited to a small number of informational workshops. The lack of funding and security cooperation is especially concerning because India is another country with a fast-growing nuclear program. According to the 2015 *Global Fissile Material Report*, India is expanding its uranium enrichment capabilities, building two new plutonium production reactors and a new reprocessing plant. India's new "fast breeder" reactor is expected to produce 140 kilograms of plutonium a year. "India has taken significant measures to protect its nuclear sites, but recent reports suggest some nuclear security weaknesses,"[22] Bunn, Malin, Roth, and Tobey add.

The weakness of India's security was on display when heavily armed members of the Jaish-e-Mohammed terrorist group in Pakistan crossed into India and infiltrated the Pathankot Air Force Base in January 2016. The terrorists defeated the base's security perimeter simply by climbing a eucalyptus tree that had grown next to the base's 11-foot-high (3.4-m) wall and jumping into the restricted area. The attackers killed seven Indian security guards and soldiers before being subdued after a three-day firefight.

Sabotage in Belgium ■

Developing nations are not the only ones that have experienced nuclear security breakdowns. Determined individuals have managed to breach nuclear security in highly developed countries as well. A frightening example occurred in Belgium in August 2014. A still unidentified person inside the Doel-4 nuclear power plant secretly opened a locked valve and drained all the lubricant from one of the plant's turbines. Without lubrication, the turbine overheated and was destroyed. The sabotage occurred in a nonnuclear area of the plant, so no radioactive material was released. However, the incident serves as an example of how a terrorist might be able to destroy part of a nuclear power plant from the inside and release radioactive material into the air, endangering civilians and causing a panic.

Concerns about a terrorist infiltrating a nuclear power plant are genuine. The investigation that followed the sabotage at the

A Small-Time Smuggler Moves Weapons-Grade Uranium

At about one thirty in the morning on June 26, 2003, a radiation detector at a border checkpoint in Georgia beeped. As guards approached, the man going through the checkpoint threw his leather satchel on the ground and surrendered. The guards searched the bag and found a metal box containing a plastic bag filled with a green powder. The contraband was later identified as HEU.

The smuggler, an Armenian trader named Garik Dadayan, professed ignorance. He said the bag was for carrying food, and he had never seen the substance inside. His personal notebook told a different story. It contained a note about uranium 308, along with a sum of money that Dadayan was to receive for moving the weapons-grade uranium across the Georgian border and into Armenia. The Georgian officials handed Dadayan over to the Armenian authorities. Dadayan, a veteran of Armenia's war with Azerbaijan who suffers from physical and mental disabilities, was tried in Armenia. He was found guilty and sentenced to two and a half years in prison.

Dadayan received a light sentence because he was believed to be nothing more than a low-level courier, or mule. "The deal to smuggle the bomb-grade uranium, according to the Georgians, reportedly involved a corrupt Russian military officer, elements of the Georgian and Armenian criminal underworlds, and an Armenian contact of Kurdish descent working in Russia," wrote journalist Lawrence Scott Sheets. Everyone was bribed, except for the border guards who caught the smugglers.

Lawrence Scott Sheets, "A Smuggler's Story," *Atlantic*, April 2008. www.theatlantic.com.

Belgian Doel-4 nuclear power plant turned up a chilling fact: Two years before the incident, a contractor working at Doel-4 with high-level security clearance quit his job and traveled to Syria to join the IS. The contractor, Ilyass Boughalab, inspected welds inside the plant. His security clearance gave him access to areas of the plant that involved nuclear materials. Because Boughalab had left the plant two years before the turbine sabotage, he was not a suspect in the incident. However, he belonged to an organization called Sharia4Belgium and was later convicted of terrorist activities related to the group. Boughalab's family said he was radicalized after receiving his security clearance, but he was still working at the power plant when he became affiliated with Sharia4Belgium. His presence in the most restricted areas of the facility dramatizes the difficulty of maintaining security in nuclear facilities.

Another terrorist plot targeting Belgian nuclear facilities was discovered after the November 2015 Paris terrorist attacks that left 130 people dead. Belgian police searching the home of Mohamed Bakkali, one of the IS terrorists arrested after the attacks, found surveillance footage tracking the movements of a Belgian nuclear official. The purpose of the surveillance was not clear, but experts believe it could have been part of a plot to abduct the official, who had access to secure areas of a nuclear research facility in Mol, Belgium. The terrorists might have tortured the intended victim or threatened his family to force him to turn over radioactive material to be used in a nuclear bomb.

Attacking Nuclear Facilities via Computer ■

Terrorists do not have to be present inside a nuclear facility to damage it and release radioactive materials. It is possible to seize control of a nuclear facility through its computer system and create havoc. Nuclear facilities already have been the targets of cyberattacks. A malicious computer worm known as Stuxnet was introduced into Iran's Natanz centrifuge facility sometime before 2010, and it took control of the centrifuges used to enrich uranium. The Stuxnet worm caused the centrifuges to spin so fast that they tore themselves apart, destroying about one-fifth of Iran's nuclear centrifuges. The worm most likely was introduced into the Natanz computer system from the inside via a memory stick.

The cyberattack on Iran's nuclear facility was not an isolated incident. On the contrary, such attacks have become common. An insider placed a virus in the computers of a Lithuanian nuclear power plant in 1992. In 2014 hackers—probably based in North Korea—broke into the computer systems of the South Korean nuclear plant operator, although they

WORDS IN CONTEXT

worm

a stand-alone malware computer program that is capable of replicating itself in order to spread to other computers

Technicians monitor systems at the Bushehr Nuclear Power Plant in Iran. In 2010 a computer worm attacked another Iranian nuclear facility, proving cyberattacks on such facilities are a reality. Viruses and worms can steal nuclear secrets or even cause machinery within the plants to obey outside commands.

did not gain control of the reactor control systems. A number of incidents have taken place at US nuclear power plants as well, including some that rendered systems important to safety inoperable for hours. "Cyberattacks on nuclear facilities have happened," says Anno Keizer, vice chair of the Working Group on Managing Cyber Threat at the Nuclear Industry Summit. "It is not a fantasy; it is not a hypothetical situation; it's what happens in real life and which we need to manage in real life. We have also seen that the consequences of an attack can be substantial, both in damaging equipment and disturbing the services that the company delivers to society."[23]

Hacking into Weapons Systems ■
Hacking could provide an opening for terrorists to achieve the ultimate act of sabotage—using a nuclear weapon in a terrorist

attack. Nuclear weapons sites are protected from physical intrusion by many layers of defense, including exterior barriers, perimeter sensors, video surveillance, and physical identification systems. However, the computers controlling such sites might not be as secure. A US Department of Defense task force reported in 2013, "Our nuclear deterrent is regularly evaluated for reliability and readiness. However most of the systems have not been assessed (end-to-end) against a . . . [high-level] cyber attack to understand possible weak spots."[24] General C. Robert Kehler, then head of US Strategic Command, found the report disturbing. He told the Senate that he was "very concerned with the potential of a cyberrelated attack on our nuclear command and control and on the weapons systems themselves."[25]

Many of the world's long-range nuclear missiles are located on submarines. Defense officials assume that such arsenals are safe

The USS John Warner (pictured) is part of the American nuclear submarine fleet. A number of nations possess subs that can fire nuclear warheads. Critics argue that the subs are susceptible to hacking because they receive radio communications.

from cyberattack because they are air gapped; that is, they are not directly connected to the Internet. Andrew Futter, senior lecturer in international politics at the University of Leicester in the United Kingdom, does not believe the submarines are as secure as commonly believed. He writes that nuclear armed submarines are susceptible to hacking because they regularly receive radio communications. "There is evidence that hackers have attempted to compromise the extremely low frequency radio communications used to send launch approval messages to US nuclear-armed submarines in the past," Futter writes. "It must be assumed that the same is true for the communications hub for British . . . [nuclear submarines] based at Northwood in the Chiltern Hills."[26] Since the submarines are not completely isolated from unsecured networks, Futter concludes: "It will never be possible to say that the UK nuclear deterrent is entirely safe from cyber attack, or that it cannot be compromised or undermined in some other way in the future."[27]

WORDS IN CONTEXT

air gapped

a security measure that physically isolates a computer or group of computers from unsecured networks, such as the Internet

While much progress has been made in nuclear security, gaps remain in the infrastructure, the procedures, and the reliability of the human beings involved in nuclear security. Engineering solutions are needed to close these gaps.

CHAPTER 3

SOLUTIONS:
Safeguarding or Eliminating Nuclear Materials

"Because there is no effective protection against nuclear terrorism, the only solution is to prevent terrorists from obtaining nuclear weapons, and the fissile materials needed to make them, in the first place."

—Union of Concerned Scientists

Union of Concerned Scientists, "Preventing Nuclear Terror Fact Sheet," April 2004. www.ucsusa.org.

The world is awash in weapons-grade nuclear materials. According to the International Panel on Fissile Materials (IPFM), the United States and Russia together possess more 1,278 metric tons of HEU. That is enough HEU to make more than one hundred thousand atom bombs, according to the Union of Concerned Scientists. The United States alone has 95.4 metric tons of plutonium—enough to make more than forty-four thousand hydrogen bombs. Terrorists do not need to build tens of thousands of nuclear bombs to terrorize their enemies. One bomb would create unimaginable fear. A handful of bombs could be used to blackmail governments into submitting to virtually any terrorist demands. Preventing terrorists from obtaining fissile materials is the second-highest antiterrorism priority, surpassed only by stopping extremists from getting actual, finished weapons.

The surest way to keep terrorists from gaining control of fissile material is to eliminate it. Security systems can be defeated, but if the material does not exist, it cannot be used to make a weapon. Weapons-grade material can be destroyed by changing its molecular structure so it is not usable for making bombs. Any nuclear material not destroyed must be secured. This includes consolidating nuclear materials into fewer locations that can be better defended and strengthening security at the remaining nuclear sites. Improving security might include limiting human access to the radioactive materials by replacing workers with robots, employing more advanced monitoring systems for nuclear laboratories and power plants, and creating a database of security breaches of nuclear facilities.

Ceasing Plutonium Production ■

The first step toward ridding the world of weapons-grade nuclear material is to stop producing more of it. Burning uranium fuel in a nuclear power plant creates plutonium as a by-product. Although the plutonium is mixed with spent uranium fuel, it can be separated, or reprocessed, for use in nuclear weapons. "We all know the problem," Barack Obama told an audience at Hankuk University in Seoul, South Korea, in 2012. "The very process that gives us nuclear energy can also put nations and terrorists within the reach of nuclear weapons. We simply can't go on accumulating huge amounts of the very material, like separated plutonium, that we're trying to keep away from terrorists."[28]

One way to slow the production of plutonium is to require nuclear power plants to use a "once-through" fuel cycle in which the plutonium remains mixed with the highly radioactive spent uranium fuel. This process keeps plutonium from being available for use in a nuclear weapon. "The United States and other interested countries should seek to ensure that . . . no more plutonium is reprocessed each year than is used, bringing global plutonium stocks down over time,"[29] recommend experts at the Harvard Kennedy School.

Changing the fuel process in the world's nuclear power plants would require both diplomatic and engineering efforts. Diplomacy would be needed to persuade nations to switch to a once-through fuel cycle. This most likely would require providing financial incentives to do so, since separated plutonium has a financial value, and many nations would not want to give it up. Nations that agree to abandon the "closed" fuel cycle would have to allow monitoring of their nuclear facilities to ensure the process is being followed. A possible engineering solution to prevent the

An American nuclear bomb disposal unit dismantles a bomb designed to be carried by aircraft. The US Department of Energy's National Nuclear Security Administration is responsible for removing such weapons and safely stowing the nuclear payloads.

unauthorized production of plutonium would be the development of a radiation monitoring system that could transmit real-time data on the reactor's contents to an impartial international organization such as the IAEA. Such a monitoring device could detect signs that the reactor was being operated in a way to maximize the production of plutonium rather than the production of power. It could also detect the removal of any amount of plutonium from a nuclear reactor site.

Downblending HEU and Plutonium ■

At the same time diplomats are working to stop the production of weapons-grade nuclear material, chemical and nuclear engineers can work to degrade the existing materials so they can no longer be used to make nuclear weapons. To accomplish this task, engineers combine the HEU or plutonium with other chemical elements in a way that lowers the purity of the nuclear material.

This process is known as downblending. US law defines uranium downblending as "processing highly enriched uranium into a uranium product in any form in which the uranium contains less than 20 percent uranium-235."[30] Plutonium is typically downblended to a concentration of less than 10 percent by weight. According to the IPFM, as of the end of 2014, the United States had downblended 146.1 metric tons of HEU, turning it into low-enriched uranium (LEU), and Russia had downblended 517 metric tons. In addition, through 2009 the United States had used or downblended 14 metric tons of plutonium, turning it into mixed oxides.

Downblended weapons-grade materials cannot be used to make a nuclear bomb, but they can be used as fuel in commercial nuclear power plants. LEU already is used as nuclear fuel. Plutonium mixed with depleted uranium creates a substance known as mixed oxide (MOX) fuel that can also be used in nuclear power generation. However, converting downblended plutonium to nuclear fuel is a highly technical and extremely expensive process. In 2007 the US government began to build the nation's first and only facility for turning surplus plutonium into MOX fuel at the government's Savannah River nuclear reservation in South Carolina. Although patterned after a working facility in France, the MOX Fuel Fabrication Plant has presented many challenges. The plant was estimated to cost $4.9 billion to build and was scheduled to begin operation in 2016. However, in 2012 the US Government Accountability Office revised the estimated cost up to $7.7 billion and said the plant would not start up before 2019. Many experts now oppose completing the facility. "The MOX program has veered off on the wrong track," states the Union of Concerned Scientists. "Every dollar spent on finishing construction and installing equipment in the MOX plant that may never be used is a wasted dollar, and moves a potential repurposing of the structure further out of reach."[31]

Some experts believe it makes more sense to downblend plutonium to an even lower level of purity and dispose of it at the Waste Isolation Pilot Plant (WIPP) near Carlsbad, New Mexico, which opened in 1999 and has already disposed of several tons of plutonium. "Permanent disposal . . . through down-blending and disposal in WIPP guarantees non-proliferation, forever,"[32] writes John Heaton, the chair of the Carlsbad Mayor's Nuclear Task Force.

Immobilization ■

While downblending is the most effective way to prevent terrorists from obtaining weapons-grade material, it is costly and technologically difficult to do. A simpler, low-tech way of safeguarding weapons-grade material is to surround it with heavy material that makes it more difficult to move and steal—a technique known as immobilization. Nuclear pellets used as fuel in nuclear reactors are usually the size and shape of a stack of four or five nickels.

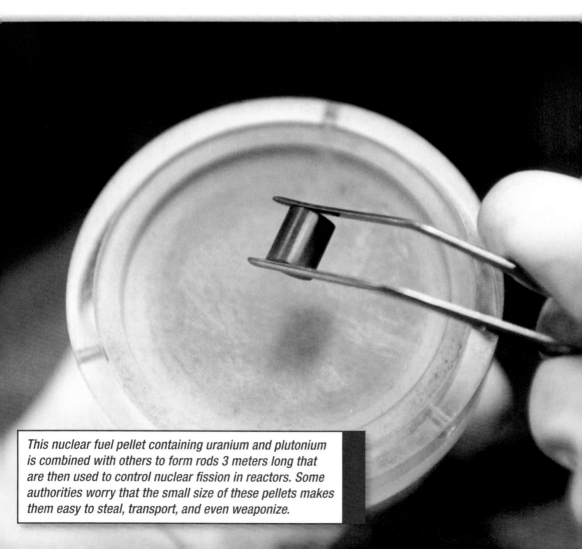

This nuclear fuel pellet containing uranium and plutonium is combined with others to form rods 3 meters long that are then used to control nuclear fission in reactors. Some authorities worry that the small size of these pellets makes them easy to steal, transport, and even weaponize.

A handful of nuclear pellets could easily fit in a metal tube that shields a smuggler from their radiation and is small enough to be carried in a trouser pocket, purse, or laptop bag. Meanwhile, the plutonium core of a nuclear weapon, known as the pit, is about the size of a billiard ball and weighs between three and four kilograms, making it relatively easy to conceal and move. Unlike uranium, plutonium does not release dangerous levels of radiation. "Theft of plutonium is a serious risk because the amount of plutonium needed to make a crude nuclear bomb is small and light enough to be easily carried and does not pose an immediate risk of severe injury to the thief," writes the Union of Concerned Scientists. "Immobilization or downblending are the only technologies clearly capable of handling the bulk of the current and projected future inventories of excess plutonium."[33]

> ## WORDS IN CONTEXT
>
> ### immobilization
>
> a method of safeguarding weapons-grade material that involves surrounding that material with something heavy to foil attempted theft

The DOE has approved an immobilization technique known as can-in-canister. In this solution, nuclear engineers mix a small amount of plutonium with ceramic material to form a hockey puck–sized disk. The engineers stack the ceramic disks inside metal canisters that are about 2 feet (61 cm) high. When fully loaded, each canister holds about one kilogram of plutonium mixed in with the ceramic material. The engineers arrange twenty-eight of these canisters inside a larger metal container, 2 feet (61 cm) in diameter and 10 feet (3 m) high. They then fill the large container with molten glass containing highly radioactive waste. After the glass cools and solidifies, the canister is sealed and placed in a nuclear storage site. The size, weight, and radioactivity of the containers serve as a barrier to theft.

Consolidation ■

The United States and Russia have agreed to downblend or immobilize 34 metric tons of plutonium each. However, neither government has agreed to destroy all of its weapons-grade material. For example, in its 2014 declaration to the IAEA, the United States reported that it had 95.4 metric tons of plutonium. The government added that the majority of that plutonium—61.5 metric tons—was not needed for national security. The government is disposing of the surplus material. Nevertheless, it plans to keep about 33.9 metric tons for military purposes. Russia and other countries do not intend to destroy or immobilize all of their weapons-grade material, either.

The best way of keeping the remaining weapons-grade materials away from terrorists is to consolidate the dangerous material into the smallest number of sites as possible. Fewer sites means smaller perimeters that need to be guarded, less square footage inside facilities that need to be monitored, and fewer human beings with access to the weapons, materials, and computer systems. The security experts at the Harvard Kennedy School write:

> Global stocks of civilian separated plutonium are immense, but few current efforts are targeted either on minimizing these huge stocks or reducing the number of locations where they are stored and handled. . . . Each country with nuclear weapons, HEU, or separated plutonium should undertake a review of each site where these materials exist, eliminating any site whose continued benefits are outweighed by its costs and risks.[34]

Some policy analysts believe the United States should take an active role in consolidating the world's nuclear material. Over the past few decades, the United States has supplied many other nations with HEU and plutonium to use in research facilities. Experts at the Harvard Kennedy School have called on the US government to reclaim those materials as a way of consolidating the world's supply of weapons-grade material. "Current U.S. plans for HEU removals would leave tons of U.S.-origin HEU in foreign countries (primarily in Europe)," write analysts at the Harvard Kennedy School. "The U.S. government should have a blanket policy that wherever plutonium or HEU exists in the world, it will . . . take it back to be secured in the United States."[35]

Consolidation applies not only to enriched nuclear material, but also to spent nuclear fuel. While spent fuel cannot be used to make a nuclear bomb, terrorists could target it to create the effects of a dirty bomb. Nuclear waste is especially vulnerable because much

Sealing Nuclear Waste in Salt

A 250-million-year-old salt deposit might be the future home of America's nuclear waste. Congress passed a law designating Yucca Mountain, Nevada, as the site for disposing of nuclear waste generated by civilian power plants, but the storage project was halted in 2009. Meanwhile, the federal government has been disposing of nuclear waste in a giant salt deposit located twenty-six miles outside Carlsbad, New Mexico. Opened in 1999, the Waste Isolation Pilot Plant (WIPP) holds more than 85,000 cubic meters of radioactive waste generated by government weapons programs. The storage vaults are located 2,150 feet (655 m) under the surface of the salt deposit. Unlike rock, salt flows under pressure. The storage rooms at WIPP are already closing in at the rate of two to three inches per year. The idea is for the nuclear waste to be completely swallowed up and encrusted by the salt, keeping it from polluting the environment and making it inaccessible to nuclear terrorists. "Our design is centered around accentuating and speeding the process of closure, encapsulation, and re-annealing [the process of chemical bonding as the salts join together again]," explains Ned Elkins, WIPP program manager for Los Alamos National Laboratory. With Yucca Mountain on hold, experts are looking at expanding WIPP so it can accept non–weapons related nuclear waste.

Quoted in Jessica Morrison, "A Salty Solution for Nuclear Waste," Nova Next, August 27, 2013. www.pbs .org/wgbh/nova/next/tech/solving-nuclear-waste-with-wipp/.

of it is stored outdoors at the nuclear power plants where it was generated. Some of it remains in ponds where the fuel rods containing it were placed to cool. Some is stored in metal containers known as dry casks. According to the IPFM, at the end of 2014 the United States had an estimated 625 metric tons of plutonium mixed with other materials stored at nuclear power plants.

Terrorists could attack these storage sites with conventional explosives, either by planting a bomb inside the facility or by striking the waste with a shoulder-launched missile. Such an attack would scatter the radioactive material into the atmosphere as a type of dirty bomb.

Challenges to Consolidation ■

While the concept of consolidating nuclear waste is simple, its execution is complicated. Engineers must meet several challenges relating to safety issues. They must design ways to safely house, move, and store the radioactive materials, including protecting them from terrorist attack.

The first issue facing engineers is how to encase the material so it will not leak radiation after an accident or attack. Currently, nuclear pellets are housed in nuclear fuel rods. After the fuel has been used up, or spent, the rods are cooled in a pond of water. Sometimes the rods are then placed in large metal containers known as nuclear fuel shipping casks. In the United States the design of nuclear shipping casks is regulated by federal law, but these standards are focused on surviving accidents rather than withstanding terrorist attacks. For example, a cask must be able to withstand being surrounded by fire of 1,475 degrees Fahrenheit (802°C) for thirty minutes. However, terrorists might be able to create and sustain a fire with temperatures higher than that. Shipping casks also must be able to withstand being submerged in 655 feet (200 m) of water for one hour or immersed in 3 feet (91 cm) of water for eight hours. This does not account for the possibility of terrorists dropping a commandeered cask into deeper water off the shores of a city such as New York or San Francisco, where it might implode, polluting the water with nuclear waste. By law, casks must be able to withstand a 30-foot (9-m) fall onto a flat, unyielding surface and a 39-inch (99-cm) fall onto a steel rod 6 inches (15 cm) in diameter. The last requirement is designed to ensure the outer casing will not be punctured during a train derailment or vehicle collision. However, there are no standard tests for the spent fuel casks surviving an attack by explosives or armor-piercing projectiles, which could exceed the force of falling from the prescribed heights.

Charles D. Ferguson, a senior fellow for science and technology at the Council on Foreign Relations, thinks the failure to design nuclear casks to withstand terrorist attacks is an important vulnerability. In 2007 Australia's *Sunday Morning Herald* reported that a group of terrorists had stolen Australian army rocket launchers with the intention of attacking a nuclear reactor in Sydney. Ferguson believes the small missiles would not do significant damage to the nuclear reactor, which is housed deep inside a concrete-and-steel structure. However, he worries about the effect the missiles could have on nuclear materials shipping casks: "The Australian Defense Forces have dozens of shoulder-fired Javelin 'fire-and-forget' missiles that have lock-on targeting and infra-red guidance, and such a long-range and highly penetrating missile fired more than a kilometer away could have penetrated the relatively thin shell of the shipping casks."[36] Designing a cask that can withstand missile attacks is a structural engineering challenge that has not been met.

Engineers also must anticipate that terrorists might attempt to steal the nuclear waste casks while they are being transported. In the United States, the Nuclear Regulatory Commission (NRC) currently requires carriers of nuclear shipping casks to provide armed security in heavily populated areas but not throughout the

Because terrorists might target vehicles transporting nuclear materials, regulatory agencies make certain that these shipments are well-guarded by security teams and that other safety measures are in place. Despite precautions, though, the risks are never eliminated.

journey. This leaves a gap in security. The NRC also requires carriers to follow only approved routes, to use devices to immobilize the casks during transport, to monitor the casks using redundant communications, and to give advance notice to the NRC and states through which the shipments will pass. In the United Kingdom regulations call for trains conveying nuclear waste to be hauled by two locomotives—one to pull the train and one for backup, in case the first engine fails.

Security engineering, a specialized field of engineering that focuses on the security aspects in the design of systems, could be employed to make transportation of nuclear materials more secure than current regulations do. For example, security engineers might design systems that meet notification regulations but

A Private Sector Solution

With the Yucca Mountain nuclear waste storage facility on hold and the expansion of the Waste Isolation Pilot Plant years away, a private company has requested permission to build and maintain a temporary nuclear waste storage site in Andrews County, Texas. In April 2016, Waste Control Specialists (WCS), a company that treats and disposes of radioactive and hazardous waste, applied to the NRC for a license to build and maintain a temporary storage site for used nuclear fuel. Plans call for the material to be housed in a 7-foot (2-m) thick, steel-reinforced concrete liner embedded in a 1,200-foot (366-m) thick red clay formation. The facility is designed to store 5,000 metric tons of spent nuclear fuel received from commercial nuclear power reactors across the United States. WCS president Rod Baltzer says the facility would require a year to construct and could become operational in 2021. At its peak, the facility should be able to receive more than 150 shipments of waste a year. "WCS anticipates that all of the fuel will arrive by rail in highly tested and extremely safe transport casks," Baltzer stated at a February 2017 public hearing. The safety review will require twenty-one months to complete, with a final licensing decision to come in 2019.

Quoted in Sam Kaufman, "Hearing Draws Nuclear Opponents from Far Away," *Andrews County (TX) News*, February 19, 2017, p. 5.

require the notified individuals to keep the times and routes of radiation shipments secret. Keeping the shipping schedules secret would make it more difficult for terrorists or saboteurs to plan an attack. In addition, security engineers might create a system in which trains and trucks are loaded with empty casks that serve as decoys. A larger number of casks being sent to multiple locations would confuse saboteurs and terrorists who might be planning an attack on the radioactive material, lowering the odds of their success.

Safe Storage of Nuclear Waste ■

Once the engineering challenges of transportation have been met, questions would remain about where the consolidated materials could be safely stored. Twenty-five years of research and $4 billion worth of testing and development by the DOE led Congress to designate Yucca Mountain in Nevada as a repository for waste from nuclear power plants. Obama put the Yucca Mountain plan on hold in 2009. If the Yucca Mountain facility is not revived, a great deal of engineering will be required to find a new location for the materials and to design a new storage facility.

Finding a safe location to consolidate nuclear materials involves geophysical engineering to assess the stability of the site for up to 1 million years after the facility has been closed. According to Environmental Protection Agency (EPA) rules adopted in 2009, the DOE must show that a nuclear storage facility can safely keep wastes from emitting 15 millirem or less per year for 10,000 years and 100 millirem or less per year for another 990,000 years. Engineers must consider the effects of earthquakes, volcanic activity, climate change, and corrosion on the containers for the duration of the storage. Geophysical engineers use technologies such as electromagnetics, ground-penetrating radar, and seismic refraction to study the geological structure of the site.

One of the most important concerns—one that played a part in derailing the Yucca Mountain plan—is the historical, current, and projected locations of groundwater. Water can corrode

> **WORDS IN CONTEXT**
>
> **geophysical**
>
> pertaining to a branch of earth science that deals with the physical processes and phenomena occurring in the earth

metal casks, and any radioactive leakage into the groundwater can cause environmental and health problems. Once a suitable site is chosen, civil engineers, architectural engineers, nuclear engineers, and security engineers will be required to build a storage facility and keep it secure. In the short term, the National Research Council of the National Academies of Sciences, Engineering, and Medicine recommends moving spent fuel currently stored in outdoor pools into more secure dry cask storage, making it harder for terrorists to target the nuclear material.

The ultimate engineering solution for safeguarding nuclear material would be not just to consolidate and downblend it, but to stop producing it altogether, even for peaceful means. The replacement of the nuclear power industry with another source of energy production would eliminate the problems of nuclear power plant sabotage or attack, the theft of radioactive materials for bomb making, the safe transportation of spent fuels, and the building of secure storage facilities. However, nuclear power currently provides 11 percent of the world's energy, and more nuclear power plants are being planned. The replacement of this energy source is a long-range engineering challenge.

CHAPTER 4

SOLUTIONS: Tracking, Detecting, and Stopping the Use of Nuclear Materials

"In the war against terrorism, America's vast science and technology base provides us with a key advantage."

— President George W. Bush

George W. Bush, "Remarks by the President in Address to the Nation," White House, June 6, 2002. https:// georgewbush-whitehouse.archives.gov.

Even if nuclear engineers are able to decrease the amount of nuclear material in weapons facilities, research laboratories, and nuclear power plants, the world will not be completely safe from nuclear terrorism. Enough plutonium and HEU is already missing from known stockpiles for terrorists to fashion dozens if not hundreds of dirty bombs or even nuclear bombs. According to the IPFM, 2.4 metric tons of plutonium known to have been produced or acquired by the United States cannot be accounted for. That is enough plutonium to make more than one thousand nuclear bombs. Thousands of kilograms of plutonium and HEU also went missing when the Soviet Union, home to the world's largest stockpiles of nuclear material, dissolved into fifteen separate nations in 1991. With all the nuclear material known to be lost, antiterrorism strategies must include efforts to detect and track nuclear material. Some of these efforts can be accomplished by undercover police work and traditional spying, but the majority of it needs to be done with technology. Engineers can reduce the possibility of nuclear terror by building systems that will detect radioactive materials leaving nuclear facilities, crossing borders, and moving around nations being targeted by terrorists.

Detecting Smuggling and Theft ■

A comprehensive, end-to-end nuclear materials monitoring system would start at the facilities where nuclear material is being used and plutonium is being created as a by-product of nuclear power production. Some experts call for electronic monitoring of radiation levels within weapons, research, and nuclear power facilities. A sudden drop in radiation levels would indicate that material has been stolen by terrorists or removed by corrupt employees planning to sell the materials on the black market. These systems could feed information about the incident into a global database maintained by the IAEA, UN, or another international body. The system would alert security agencies around the world as soon as any amount of nuclear material went missing.

The same database could also be used as a learning tool after the theft has occurred. Officials could add details to the original incident reports, describing exactly how security systems were breached. Such a database could be accessed by officials at any time to train new employees or to provide support for suggested upgrades to their security systems. "Sharing of incidents . . . is routine, and extremely important, in strengthening nuclear safety," write Bunn, Malin, Roth, and Tobey. "It is time to undertake a similar approach in nuclear security. The United States should work with other states to establish a shared database of security-related incidents."[37]

The Two-Person Rule ■

Many breaches of nuclear security—the destruction of the turbine at the Belgian Doel-4 nuclear power plant, the bribery of the directors at the Siberian Chemical Combine in Russia, and the sharing of nuclear secrets with al Qaeda by Sultan Bashiruddin Mahmood—have one thing in common: They involve human beings. As Ryan Kalember, a security analyst with the cybersecurity firm Proofpoint, puts it: "People are always the weak link in the [security] chain."[38]

One way to prevent terrorists and others from stealing nuclear materials or sabotaging nuclear facilities is to employ the same human engineering principle that is used to prevent the unauthorized launch of a nuclear weapon: the two-person rule. Under this rule, no single individual is permitted access to nuclear systems or materials. Any decision or access must be agreed on by two

To limit unauthorized access to nuclear materials and prevent potential sabotage, many facilities restrict single individuals from working with or performing maintenance on nuclear devices. Instead, all labor and decisions are overseen by pairs or small groups of qualified technicians.

people. This prevents a single individual—often referred to as a lone wolf—from committing sabotage or stealing nuclear material. After Belgian authorities discovered the act of sabotage at the Doel-4 facility, they instituted the two-person rule in all of the nation's nuclear power plants.

Replacing Human Beings with Robots ∎

While the two-person rule reduces the chances of terrorism or sabotage in a nuclear facility, it is always possible for a lone wolf terrorist to overpower the second person or to convince the person to help carry out a terrorist act. A simple alternative to the two-person rule is to replace as many human workers as possible with automated systems and robots. This is not a new idea. A technical committee within the IAEA writes:

> In one form or another, robotics and automatic plant control systems have already played a vital role in the safe and economic operation of nuclear power stations . . . . Robots already replace manual actions with complicated

or dangerous access (radiation) or perform work which is boring or requires continuous attention (welding, bolting, ultrasonic inspection). Further, robots are used for [radiation risk] reduction tasks (piping, steam generator inspection, plugging) or for special purposes, where human factor problems are minimized.[39]

To guard against theft and sabotage, nuclear engineers and computer engineers could design even more automated systems, replacing additional human workers with a network of electronic sensors that provide continuous feedback to a main computer. In areas where sensors cannot be embedded into the machinery, mobile robots could move through the facility, inspecting machinery and looking for damage to the infrastructure. In 2014 engineers at the South Texas Project nuclear plant in Bay City, Texas, successfully tested a robot designed to inspect a length of buried pipe. The self-propelled robot made by GE Hitachi can inspect piping from 6 to 48 inches (15.2 to 122 cm) in diameter, negotiating tight turns and traveling up to 1,000 feet (305 m) from its entry point.

Not only can robots go deep inside nuclear facilities, they also can work high up a facility's walls. International Climbing Machines, a robotics company located in Ithaca, New York, has developed climbing robots that can inspect very large concrete structures such as nuclear power plant towers and containment buildings. The robots use vacuum suction to remain attached to surfaces. Sam Maggio, the company's president, says, "It's the vacuum chamber, which is surrounded by a rolling, very flexible seal, that allows it to go over very rough surfaces as well as surface obstacles."[40] According to the IAEA committee, "Robotic devices can be effectively used in nuclear installations to perform detailed functions pertaining to many tasks, including functions to control access to critical areas of the installation, detection of intruders or attempts to sabotage a nuclear installation."[41]

Stopping Smugglers at the Borders ■
Despite the best efforts to prevent the theft of nuclear weapons or materials, it is possible that terrorists already possess them or will obtain them before stronger security measures are put in place. The next line of defense is to prevent nuclear materials or

Kill Switches for Nuclear Weapons

Many electronic devices now come equipped with a remote "kill switch" that renders the device useless when lost or stolen, preventing the person who has the device from accessing the owner's personal information. Some engineers think such technology could be inserted into nuclear weapons to prevent their use by terrorists. Several types of kill switches have been proposed. One solution is timed expiration. With this solution, the weapon would be armed for a finite time. After the time expires, the weapon would have to receive a new electronic signal that would allow it to be used. These updates would occur regularly and automatically, but they would stop if a weapon goes missing, rendering it useless to the group that stole it.

Another solution is GPS limitations. Nations already program weapons to attack certain targets. A GPS kill switch would turn off the weapon if it were aimed at any other target, again rendering it useless to terrorists who would want to use the weapon against another target. Jonathan Zittrain, a computer science professor at Harvard University, writes:

> It is past time that we consider whether we should build in a way to remotely disable such dangerous tools in an emergency. Other technologies, including smartphones, already incorporate this kind of capability. The theft of iPhones plummeted this year after Apple introduced a remote "kill switch." . . . If this feature is worth putting in consumer devices, why not embed it in devices that can be so devastatingly repurposed?

Jonathan Zittrain, "The Case for Kill Switches in Military Weaponry," *Scientific American*, September 3, 2014. www.scientificamerican.com.

weapons from crossing borders and entering a target nation such as the United States. According to terrorism analyst Jonathan Medalia:

> If terrorists acquired a nuclear weapon, they could try many means to bring it into the United States. This nation has thousands of miles of land and sea borders, as well as

several hundred ports of entry. Terrorists might smuggle a weapon across lightly-guarded stretches of borders, ship it in using a cargo container, place it in a crude oil tanker, or bring it in using a truck, a boat, or a small airplane.[42]

One of the hardest places to detect nuclear materials is deep inside the cargo containers of ships that bring imported food, drink, clothing, electronics, and other products for American consumers. According to the US Department of Homeland Security, about 10 million cargo containers arrive in the United States each year. The containers are massive, containing up to 30 tons (27 metric tons) of imported goods. Having people thoroughly inspect every container would be costly and disruptive, slowing the movement of the imported products into the country.

One solution to helping monitor the contents of shipping containers is to develop a computerized packing simulation program that would show the shipping companies how to load containers in a way that makes it possible to inspect them quickly. To gain the cooperation of shippers, customs officials might offer the modeling software to the shipping companies for free. They could charge less for shipments that follow the computer modeling and charge more for inspections when items are arranged in a way that does not follow the recommended method.

The Nuclear Car Wash ■

Another possible way of detecting hidden nuclear materials is to deploy a radiation detection system nicknamed the "nuclear car wash." The system gets its name from the fact that cargo containers pass through a scanning system similar to the way a vehicle moves through a car wash. The nuclear car wash is more than an enhanced version of the radiation portal monitors (RPMs) that are currently deployed at border checkpoints. RPMs work by detecting radiation given off by nuclear materials that pass nearby. Because RPMs simply receive radioactive particles, they are known as passive systems. The nuclear car wash is different. It bombards the cargo container with subatomic particles known as neutrons. For this reason, the

NO SMOKING

The fleets of container ships that move through the world's ports are vulnerable to nuclear terrorism. Although port authorities routinely investigate the cargo that comes and goes, there is not enough staff or time to check every one of the containers that circulate each day.

nuclear car wash is considered active rather than passive. The neutrons it discharges are so small that they can pass through solid materials such as the container walls and the cargo inside. When neutrons strike special nuclear material such as plutonium or HEU, they cause small, controlled fission reactions. The fission reaction gives off gamma rays, a form of radiation that also can pass through the cargo and container. Sensors outside the shipping container can detect the gamma rays and alert the customs officials to the presence of nuclear material within the container.

In 2007 the Lawrence Livermore National Laboratory tested such a system. The engineers placed a 469-gram puck of triuranium octoxide powder enriched to 94.7 percent purity inside two loads simulating the density of a fully loaded shipping container: a pallet of plywood measuring 96 inches (244 cm) long by 48 inches (122 cm) wide by 60 inches (152 cm) high and a stack of steel pipes of the same dimensions. The amount of HEU the engineers tried to detect was much smaller than the IAEA's definition of a significant amount of special nuclear material, which is

Foiling Hackers

Mark Hart, an engineer at Lawrence Livermore National Laboratory, has developed a way to frustrate terrorists who obtain a stolen nuclear weapon. To use the bomb, the terrorists need to arm it using the secret permissive action links. To obtain these codes, the terrorists would have to hack the weapon's computer system or obtain them from someone who knows them. Hart's approach would foil both methods of obtaining the codes.

Currently, each component of a weapon is assigned a unique identification number. The components are linked on a digital communications network, and they are constantly verifying each other's identification. To ensure that no unauthorized person learns the identification numbers, Hart suggests using an engineering principle known as intrinsic use control (IUC). Hart's method is based on the fact that the radiation fields around the nuclear material in the weapon fluctuate in a way that can be measured. Continuous measurements of the radiation fields would generate a series of very long, completely random code numbers that makers of the weapons would not know and hackers could never discover. Hart calls the process "letting the weapon protect itself." The likelihood of anyone overriding this system is minuscule. Hart adds, "You'd have a better chance of winning both Mega Millions and Powerball on the same day than getting control of IUC-protected components."

Quoted in Brianna Bishop, "Lawrence Livermore Scientist Develops Uncrackable Code for Nuclear Weapons," Lawrence Livermore National Laboratory, November 14, 2014. www.llnl.gov.

eight kilograms of plutonium or twenty-five kilograms of HEU. The engineers not only wanted to achieve a success rate greater than 95 percent, they also wanted to limit the number of false alarms to fewer than one-tenth of 1 percent, reasoning that too many false alarms would mean the technology would not be used or customs officials would ignore its results. "These goals must be met without impacting the flow of commerce and without subjecting either the operators or the cargo to an excessive radiation dose,"[43] stated the engineers.

To conduct the test, the nuclear engineers placed the HEU sample at various depths in the plywood stack to provide neutron paths through the cargo ranging in length from 12 to 48 inches (30 to 122 cm). They also placed the HEU at a depth of 48 inches (122 cm) in the steel pipes. After a period of testing, the engineers reported success: "Results of recent experiments show that our technique is robust and likely to meet or exceed our detection and error rate goals without subjecting either the operators or the cargo to excessive radiation dose, although exact specifications and requirements have not yet been defined,"[44] reported the scientists.

A Layered System of Defense ■

The principles of the nuclear car wash could be adapted to other situations to scan things such as air cargo and airline luggage. They could also be used to inspect vehicles at border crossings or highway checkpoints located near terrorist targets such as New York City and Washington, DC. "The deployment of sensor systems even at a large number of such choke points would not guarantee the detection of [special nuclear material] in transit," writes the National Research Council. "But the deployment of a well-tested, national integrated detection network would be a powerful component of the layered homeland defense system."[45]

Passive detection systems could also be part of an integrated detection network. Some customs officials, police officers, and firefighters are already equipped with small, handheld radiation detectors. These instruments alert the first responders to the presence of radiation at the scene of an accident or fire. Current devices are designed to alert the users to the danger of radiation poisoning. They have not been designed to stop terrorism. The equipment is not sensitive enough to tell the difference between nuclear materials used for legal purposes, such as medical radiation treatment or scientific experimentation, and those used for illicit purposes, such as terrorism. However, some experts believe engineers could develop low-cost devices with the ability to tell the difference. Each type of nuclear material—LEU, HEU, and plutonium—gives off a different set of radioactive particles, known as radioisotopes. The proportions of these particles are distinctive enough to constitute a type of radioisotope "finger-

> **WORDS IN CONTEXT**
>
> **radioisotopes**
>
> atoms that contain an unstable combination of neutrons and protons and emit radiation

print" or "signature." A new generation of radiation detectors could be programmed to set off alarms in the presence of certain radioisotope signatures but not others. Such devices could be provided to law enforcement officers to use on patrol with little danger of generating false alarms or disrupting the movement of legal, low-level nuclear materials. "These instruments could form the first layer of detection defense for illicit radioisotopes,"[46] states the National Research Council. Passive radiation detectors could also be placed in drones that can access areas that police officers do not normally patrol, such as beneath bridges; above high-rise rooftops, where a dirty bomb might be deployed for maximum effect; and over marinas, where a pleasure craft armed with a nuclear weapon could be moored.

Tracking the Terrorists ■

Locating and preventing the use of a nuclear weapon involves more than detecting the presence of radioactive material. It also involves knowing who the terrorists are, where they are located, and what they are doing. Antiterrorism intelligence typically is gathered in four ways: through human assets, or spies, who infiltrate terrorist organizations and report on their activities; by electronic eavesdropping on the conversations of the terrorists; by video surveillance of the movements and actions of terrorists; and by using computers and software programs to analyze social media and other data to pick up clues about terrorist activity.

Traditional spying with human beings can be very effective, but it is difficult to carry out against terrorist organizations. Spy organizations usually infiltrate a group by compromising an existing member of the organization. Sometimes this is done by appealing to the conscience of the individual, convincing him or her that the cause of the organization is not just. Sometimes it is accomplished by offering the person money. These techniques can work with a person who is simply doing a job, such as a government employee who is not particularly loyal to the government or its leaders, but they rarely succeed with terrorists, who are deeply committed to the group's cause. As a result, human assets are of little use in penetrating terrorist cells and preventing attacks. Instead, intelligence-gathering agencies rely on technology to uncover terrorist activities.

Electronic eavesdropping is one of the most common and effective methods of tracking terrorist activities. The US government currently has seven Advance Orion spy satellites orbiting Earth. Each satellite is equipped with a mesh antenna larger than a football field that is designed to intercept mobile phone communications of all kinds—voice, text, and pictures. The number of intercepted messages is far too great for even thousands of human beings to monitor them. Instead, analysts at the National Security Agency (NSA), the agency that interprets the satellite data, use sophisticated software to analyze the transmissions. "The foreign signals that NSA collects are invaluable to national security," the NSA declared in a 2013 statement. "This information helps the agency determine where adversaries are located, what they're planning, when they're planning to carry it out, with whom they're working, and the kinds of weapons they're using."[47]

Some first responders are receiving training in the use of radiation-detecting wands. While these devices are meant to warn first responders against contaminated sites and accidental spills, they are not currently calibrated to locate and identify weaponized nuclear materials.

In addition to intercepting messages, the NSA is able to track terrorists using the Global Positioning System (GPS) signals emitted by their mobile phones. Phones can be tracked even if the GPS function is turned off, according to a 2013 article in the *Washington Post*. "By September 2004, a new NSA technique enabled the agency to find cellphones even when they were turned off," writes reporter Dana Priest. "JSOP [Joint Special Operations Command] troops called this 'The Find,' and it gave them thousands of new targets, including members of a burgeoning al-Qaeda-sponsored insurgency in Iraq, according to members of the unit."[48]

Monitoring Cell Phone and Internet Activity ■

Electronic eavesdropping, GPS tracking, and video surveillance are also conducted within the United States. In April 2016 Peter Aldhous and Charles Seife of the Internet news organization BuzzFeed reported that flight records assembled by the flight-tracking website Flightradar24 showed that roughly two hundred federal aircraft are routinely used for surveillance within the United States. "Each weekday, dozens of U.S. government aircraft take to the skies and slowly circle over American cities," write Aldhous and Seife. According to the report, the planes fly about 1 mile (1.6 km) above the ground and use exhaust mufflers to reduce the sound of their engines and make them less noticeable. Piloted by agents of the FBI and the US Department of Homeland Security, the planes are equipped with high-resolution video cameras. "At least a few planes have carried devices that can track the cell phones of people below,"[49] add the reporters. The FBI and US Department of Homeland Security did not comment on the BuzzFeed story, but in 2015 FBI deputy director Mark Giuliano issued a statement about aircraft surveillance: "It should come as no surprise that the FBI uses planes to follow terrorists, spies, and serious criminals. We have an obligation to follow those people who want to hurt our country and its citizens, and we will continue to do so."[50]

In addition to calling and texting, terrorists also communicate with each other over the Internet. As a result, the NSA also monitors Internet activity, especially social media activity on websites such as Facebook, Twitter, Instagram, Tumblr, Snapchat, and YouTube. As with mobile phone transmissions, the volume of social media comments, shares, and posts is so great that it cannot be monitored by human beings or even normal computer programs. For example, Twitter users post an average of 500 million tweets per day. Instagram users upload more than 42 million photos a day, and YouTube users share an average of 432,000 hours of video per day. Such vast amounts of information being created so quickly is known as Big Data. Computer engineers are developing new formulas, or algorithms, to make sense of Big Data, but even more progress needs to be made. For example, terrorists can share plans by posting images bearing messages to Instagram, rather than by using the more easily searchable text messages in Twitter or Facebook. High-speed image recognition software is needed to "read" the content in these images. The same is true for videos. Facial recognition software is being developed that can lip-read videos to conduct high-speed searches of the language content, but such programs need to be improved. In addition, terrorists might show a blank screen or unrelated images while sharing an audio message. Voice recognition software, which converts audio signals to text, and natural language processing, which uses dictionaries and rules of grammar to understand the meaning of text, can be used to conduct high-speed searches of audio files to uncover terrorist plots.

> **WORDS IN CONTEXT**
>
> **algorithm**
>
> a set of steps or operations that are followed in order to solve a mathematical problem or to complete a computer process

Commitment and Action ■

The technology exists to virtually eliminate the threat of nuclear terror. Existing stockpiles of nuclear weapons can be consolidated into fewer, more secure sites. Research reactors can be converted from using weapons-grade nuclear material to using low-enriched uranium. Nuclear power plants can use once-through fuel cycles to stop producing more plutonium. Nuclear waste can be consolidated into secure disposal sites that cannot be targeted by terrorists. Surplus weapons-grade material can be downblended so it cannot be used to make a bomb. Radiation detection networks can be established that would alert authorities to the movement of nuclear materials across borders and within target countries. And terrorists themselves can be tracked and monitored so their plots can be uncovered and stopped.

Although technically possible, these efforts would require additional engineering innovations, more money, and greater cooperation between the nations of the world. The question is: Will world leaders take the threat of nuclear terrorism seriously enough to take the steps necessary to prevent it? Some experts are doubtful. Bunn, Malin, Roth, and Tobey point out that many government officials believe their nations' security measures are sufficient and they do not need to do more to stop nuclear terrorism. They write: "Complacency is the enemy of action. Unless policymakers believe that nuclear terrorism is a real and serious threat to their own countries' security, and that improvements in the aspects of nuclear security they control can significantly reduce the risk, they are unlikely to take the actions needed to address the threat."[51]

WORDS IN CONTEXT

natural language processing

the ability of a computer program to understand human speech as it is spoken

SOURCE NOTES

INTRODUCTION
An Ominous Threat

1. Ban Ki-moon, "Statement Attributable to the Spokesperson for the Secretary-General on the Entry into Force of the International Convention for the Suppression of Acts of Nuclear Terrorism," United Nations, June 13, 2007. www.un.org.
2. Osama bin Laden, "Jihad Against Jews and Crusaders," Federation of American Scientists, February 23, 1998. https://fas.org.
3. Quoted in Rolf Mowatt-Larssen, "Al Qaeda's Pursuit of Weapons of Mass Destruction," *Foreign Policy*, January 25, 2010. http://foreignpolicy.com.
4. Quoted in Heather Saul, "ISIS Claims It Could Buy Its First Nuclear Weapon from Pakistan Within a Year," *Independent* (London), May 22, 2015. www.independent.co.uk.
5. Kofi Annan, "Secretary-General Offers Global Strategy for Fighting Terrorism, in Address to Madrid Summit," press release, United Nations, March 10, 2005. www.un.org.

CHAPTER 1
CURRENT STATUS: Blocking the Pathway to a Bomb

6. Matthew Bunn et al., *Preventing Nuclear Terrorism: Continuous Improvement or Dangerous Decline?* Cambridge, MA: Belfer Center for Science and International Affairs, 2016, p. 1. http://belfercenter.ksg.harvard.edu.
7. International Atomic Energy Agency, "Convention on the Physical Protection of Nuclear Material." www.iaea.org.
8. Quoted in United Nations, "Security Council Calls for World Free of Nuclear Weapons During Historic Summit," September 24, 2009. www.un.org.
9. Quoted in Global Security News Wire, "Pakistan Says 25,000 Guards Watching Nukes," June 25, 2013. www.nti.org.

10. Lawrence J. Korb, "The Security of Pakistan's Nuclear Arsenal," *Bulletin of the Atomic Scientists*, May 19, 2009. http://thebulletin.org.
11. Bunn et al., Preventing Nuclear Terrorism, p. 40.
12. Yukiya Amano, "Speech at International Conference on Nuclear Security: Enhancing Global Efforts," International Atomic Energy Agency, July 1, 2013. www-pub.iaea.org.

CHAPTER 2
PROBLEMS: Identifying Gaps in Security

13. Quoted in Will Dunham, "Kerry Condemns Russia's 'Incredible Act of Aggression' in Ukraine," Reuters, March 2, 2014. www.reuters.com.
14. Council on Foreign Relations, "Loose Nukes," January 1, 2006. www.cfr.org.
15. Bunn et al., *Preventing Nuclear Terrorism*, p. v.
16. Quoted in Andrew Denton, "Interview of Hamid Mir on Enough Rope," ABC, March 22, 2004. www.abc.net.au.
17. Quoted in Bunn et al., *Preventing Nuclear Terrorism*, p. 82.
18. Quoted in David E. Sanger, "Obama's Worst Pakistan Nightmare," *New York Times*, January 8, 2009. www.nytimes.com.
19. Quoted in Sanger, "Obama's Worst Pakistan Nightmare."
20. Quoted in Sanger, "Obama's Worst Pakistan Nightmare."
21. Bunn et al., *Preventing Nuclear Terrorism*, p. iv.
22. Bunn et al., *Preventing Nuclear Terrorism*, p. 82.
23. Quoted in Jim Randle, "Hackers Attacking More and More Nuclear Facilities, Report Shows," Voice of America, March 31, 2016. www.voanews.com.
24. Quoted in Timothy Farnsworth, "Study Sees Cyber Risk for U.S. Arsenal," *Arms Control Today*, April 2, 2013. www.armscontrol.org.
25. Quoted in Defense Science Board, *Resilient Military Systems and the Advanced Cyber Threat*. Washington, DC: US Department of Defense, 2014, p. 7.
26. Andrew Futter, *Is Trident Safe from Cyber Attack?* London: European Leadership Network, 2016, p. 4. www.europeanleadershipnetwork.org.

27. Quoted in Levi Winchester, "Terrifying Nuke Warning: Nuclear Weapons Could Be Hacked in Cyber Attacks," *Express* (London), February 6, 2016. www.express.co.uk.

CHAPTER 3
SOLUTIONS: Safeguarding or Eliminating Nuclear Materials

28. Barack Obama, "Remarks by President Obama at Hankuk University," White House, March 26, 2012. www.whitehouse.gov.
29. Bunn et al., *Preventing Nuclear Terrorism*, p. x.
30. Quoted in Cornell University Law School, "42 U.S. Code § 2297h–10a—Incentives for Additional Downblending of Highly Enriched Uranium by the Russian Federation." www.law.cornell.edu.
31. Union of Concerned Scientists, *Excess Plutonium Disposition*, December 2014, p. 8. www.ucsusa.org.
32. John Heaton, "Down-Blending Is Best for Excess Plutonium," *Carlsbad (NM) Current-Argus*, December 26, 2015. www.currentargus.com.
33. Union of Concerned Scientists, *Excess Plutonium Disposition*, p. 8.
34. Bunn et al., *Preventing Nuclear Terrorism*, p. x.
35. Bunn et al., *Preventing Nuclear Terrorism*, p. x.
36. Quoted in Abdul Mannan, *Preventing Nuclear Terrorism in Pakistan: Sabotage of a Spent Fuel Cask or a Commercial Irradiation Source in Transport.* Washington, DC: Henry L. Stimson Center, 2007, p. 6.

CHAPTER 4
SOLUTIONS: Tracking, Detecting, and Stopping the Use of Nuclear Materials

37. Bunn et al., *Preventing Nuclear Terrorism*, p. 116.
38. Quoted in Randle, "Hackers Attacking More and More Nuclear Facilities, Report Shows."
39. Technical Committee, *Safety Aspects of Nuclear Power Plant Automation and Robotics.* Vienna: International Atomic Energy Agency, 1991, p. 3.

40. Quoted in Thomas W. Overton, "Leveraging Drones and Robots for O&M Savings," *Power*, April 1, 2016. www.power mag.com.
41. Technical Committee, *Safety Aspects of Nuclear Power Plant Automation and Robotics*, p. 24.
42. Jonathan Medalia, Nuclear Terrorism: A Brief Review of Threats and Responses. Washington, D.C.: Congressional Research Service. February 10, 2005, p. 2. https://fas.org/sgp /crs/nuke/RL32595.pdf.
43. J.M. Hall et al., "The Nuclear Car Wash: Neutron Interrogation of Cargo Containers to Detect Hidden SNM," *Nuclear Instruments and Methods in Physics Research*, May 2007, p. 338.
44. Hall et al., "The Nuclear Car Wash," p. 340.
45. National Research Council, *Making the Nation Safer: The Role of Science and Technology in Countering Terrorism.* Washington, DC: National Academies Press, 2002, p. 56.
46. National Research Council, *Making the Nation Safer*, p. 56.
47. Quoted in Dana Priest, "NSA Growth Fueled by Need to Target Terrorists," *Washington Post*, July 21, 2013. www.wash ingtonpost.com.
48. Priest, "NSA Growth Fueled by Need to Target Terrorists."
49. Peter Aldhous and Charles Seife, "Spies in the Skies," BuzzFeed, April 7, 2016. www.buzzfeed.com.
50. Quoted in Federal Bureau of Investigation, "FBI Aviation Program: Purpose and Scope," press release, June 4, 2015. www.fbi.gov.
51. Bunn et al., *Preventing Nuclear Terrorism*, p. 87.

FIND OUT MORE

Books

Graham Allison, *Nuclear Terrorism: The Ultimate Preventable Catastrophe*. New York: Holt, 2005.

Jack Caravelli, *Nuclear Insecurity: Understanding the Threat from Rogue Nations and Terrorists*. Westport, CT: Praeger Security International, 2008.

Pietro Egidi, ed., *Detection of Nuclear Weapons and Materials*. New York: Nova Science, 2010.

Brian Michael Jenkins, *Will Terrorists Go Nuclear?* Amherst, NY: Prometheus, 2008.

Michael A. Levi, *On Nuclear Terrorism*. Cambridge, MA: Harvard University Press, 2007.

Jeffrey Richelson, *Defusing Armageddon: Inside NEST, America's Secret Nuclear Bomb Squad*. New York: Norton, 2009.

Websites

Homeland Security Affairs (www.hsaj.org). *Homeland Security Affairs* is the online journal of the Naval Postgraduate School Center for Homeland Defense and Security. It features articles on strengthening US homeland security and preventing terrorism, including nuclear terrorism.

NAE Grand Challenges for Engineering (www.engineeringchallenges.org). Created by the National Academy of Engineering, this website offers a list of the grand challenges and opportunities for engineering facing those born at the dawn of this century, including a section called Prevent Nuclear Terror.

Nuclear Threat Initiative (www.nti.org). The Nuclear Threat Initiative is a nonprofit, nonpartisan organization that works to prevent catastrophic attacks with weapons of mass destruction and disruption—nuclear, biological, radiological, chemical, and cyber.

Our World in Data (https://ourworldindata.org). Developed at the University of Oxford, *Our World in Data* is an online publication that presents factual data on a wide range of contemporary issues, including sections on war and peace and terrorism. It communicates this information through interactive formats such as charts, graphs, and maps.

Internet Sources

Matthew Bunn et al., *Advancing Nuclear Security: Evaluating Progress and Setting New Goals.* Cambridge, MA: Belfer Center for Science and International Affairs, March 2014. http://belfer center.ksg.harvard.edu/files/advancingnuclearsecurity.pdf.

Matthew Bunn et al., *Preventing Nuclear Terrorism: Continuous Improvement or Dangerous Decline?* Cambridge, MA: Belfer Center for Science and International Affairs, 2016. http://belfercenter .ksg.harvard.edu/files/PreventingNuclearTerrorism-Web.pdf.

International Panel on Fissile Materials, *Global Fissile Material Report 2015*, 2015. http://fissilematerials.org/library/gfmr15.pdf.

Rolf Mowatt-Larssen, *Al Qaeda Weapons of Mass Destruction Threat: Hype or Reality?* Cambridge, MA: Belfer Center for Science and International Affairs, 2010. http://belfercenter.ksg.har vard.edu/files/al-qaeda-wmd-threat.pdf.

National Academies and US Department of Homeland Security, "Nuclear Attack," 2005. www.dhs.gov/xlibrary/assets/prep_nu clear_fact_sheet.pdf.

Barry L. Rothberg, "Averting Armageddon: Preventing Nuclear Terrorism in the United States," *Duke Journal of Comparative & International Law*, 1997. http://scholarship.law.duke.edu/cgi /viewcontent.cgi?article=1275&context=djcil.

INDEX

Note: Boldface page numbers indicate illustrations.

Advance Orion spy satellites, 63
African Nuclear-Weapon-Free Zone
    Treaty (2009), 19
air gapped, defined, 39
Aldhous, Peter, 64
algorithms, 65
Allison, Graham, 32
al-Zawahiri, Ayman, 31, 33
Annan, Kofi, 11, 16
antiballistic missiles, 18–19
antiterrorism intelligence, 62–64
atomic (A-) bombs, 21
Australia, 48

Bakkali, Mohamed, 36
Baltzer, Rod, 50
Belgium, 34–36, 55
Big Data, 64–65
bin Laden, Osama, 9, 33
biometric, defined, 24
Boughalab, Ilyass, 35–36
Bunn, Matthew
    on danger of complacency, 66
    estimated damage from detonation of
        10-kiloton weapon, 10
    on global nuclear security framework,
        27
    on HEU research reactors in Russia,
        29
    on securing nuclear stockpiles, 12
    on security situation in India, 34
    on sharing security breach
        information, 54
    on terrorist attacks on Pakistani
        facilities, 33
    on theft of weapons-grade materials
        in Russia, 20
Bush, George W., 17, 22, 53
Bushehr Nuclear Power Plant (Iran), **37**
Buzzfeed, 64

can-in-canister immobilization
    technique, 45
Cantlie, John, 9
Climbing Machines, 56
consolidation, 46–51
Convention on the Physical Protection
    of Nuclear Material and Nuclear
    Facilities (CPPNMNF), 15–16
cyberattacks, 36–39, **37**, **38**

Dadayan, Garik, 35
Dar, Ishaq, 19
diplomacy, importance of, 13
dirty bombs
    described, 22
    effects of, 9–10, 11
    strikes on storage facilities acting as,
        47
disarmament, 17, 18
Doel-4 nuclear power plant (Belgium),
    34–36, 55
downblending, 42–44
dry casks, 47

electronic eavesdropping, 63
Elkins, Ned, 47

Facebook, 64–65
facial recognition software, 65
fatwa, defined, 9
FBI, 64
Ferguson, Charles D., 48–49
fissile, defined, 13
fissile materials. *See* weapons-grade
    materials
fission bombs, 21
fission reactions, described, 59
Flightradar24 (website), 64
France, 43
Fukushima Daiichi nuclear power plant
    (Japan), 11
fusion bombs, 21
Futter, Andrew, 39

Gaidukov, Victor, 30
GE Hitachi, 56
geophysical, defined, 51
Georgia (nation), 20, 31, 35
Giuliano, Mark, 64
Global Fissile Material Report, 34
Global Initiative to Combat Nuclear
    Terrorism (GICNT), 17
global nuclear security
    current problems
        attempted smuggling or sale of
            nuclear materials, 24
        breakdown in US-Russia
            cooperation, 28
        computer attacks, 36–39, **37, 38**
        in India, 34
        Nuclear Security Summit
            termination, 31
        need to reduce number of
            storage sites of weapons-grade
            materials, 46
        in Pakistan, 32–33
        patchwork nature of measures, 27
        shipping container contents,
            57–61, **59**
        unaccounted-for plutonium, 53
        weak human link, 54–56
    international agreements/
        organizations
        African Nuclear-Weapon-Free Zone
            Treaty, 19
        Convention on the Physical
            Protection of Nuclear Material
            and Nuclear Facilities, 15–16
        Division of Nuclear Security (of
            IAEA), 15
        Global Initiative to Combat Nuclear
            Terrorism, 17
        Incident and Trafficking Database
            (of IAEA), 15, 24
        International Atomic Energy
            Agency, 15
        International Physical Protection
            Advisory Service (IPPAS, of
            IAEA), 15
        International Summit on
            Democracy, Terrorism and
            Security (2005), 11, 16
        Nuclear Security Summit, 17–18

        Treaty on the Limitation of Anti-
            Ballistic Missile Systems, 18–19
        in Pakistan, 19
        possible future measures
            computerized packing simulation
                program for shipping container,
                58
            database and monitoring of
                radiation levels in all facilities, 54
            GPS limitations, 57
            kill switches, 57
            layered, 61–62
            nuclear car washes, 58–61
            permissive action links, 60
            robots, 55–56
        in Russia, 20
Global Positioning System (GPS), 57, 64
Global Terrorism Database, 8–9
Group of Eight (G8), 16

Hart, Mark, 60
Harvard Kennedy School, 32, 41, 46
Heaton, John, 44
highly enriched uranium (HEU)
    ability to produce in India, 34
    amount possessed by US and
        Russia, 40
    attempted smuggling or sale of, 24,
        35
    downblending, 42–44
    IAEA definition of significant amount
        of, 60
    importance of, 12
    radioisotope fingerprint/signature,
        61–62
    in research reactors, 20, 29
    Russian processor of, 30–31
    used for scientific experimentation, 20
    See also weapons-grade materials
Holdren, John, 10
hydrogen (H-) bombs, 21

image recognition software, 65
immobilization, 44–45
Incident and Trafficking Database (of
    IAEA), 15, 24, 30
India
    ability to produce weapons-grade
        plutonium, 34

closed fuel cycle in power plants, 21
 security problems in, 34
Instagram, 64–65
integrated detection networks, 61–62
International Atomic Energy Agency
 (IAEA)
 attempted smuggling or sale of
  nuclear materials, 24, 30
 definition of significant amount of
  special nuclear material, 59–60
 divisions of, 15, 24
 on use of robots, 55–56
International Panel on Fissile Materials
 (IPFM)
 amount of downblended HEU in US
  and Russia, 43
 amount of downblended plutonium in
  US, 43
 amount of stored plutonium in US, 47
 number of atom bombs possible from
  weapons-grade nuclear materials in
  US and Russia, 40
 unaccounted-for plutonium, 53
International Physical Protection
 Advisory Service (IPPAS), 15
International Summit on Democracy,
 Terrorism and Security (2005), 11, 16
Internet activity, 64–65
intrinsic use control (IUC) principle, 60
Iran, 33, 36, **37**
Islamic State (IS), 9

Jaish-e-Mohammed terrorist group, 34
Japan, 8, 11
Jordan, 18

Kalember, Ryan, 54
Kehler, C. Robert, 38
Keizer, Anno, 37
Kerry, John, 28
Khan, Abdul Qadeer, 33
Khintsagov, Oleg Vladimirovich, 31
kill switches, 57
Ki-moon, Ban, 8, 9
Korb, Lawrence J., 19

Lawrence Livermore National
 Laboratory, 59–60
Lithuania, 36

low-enriched uranium (LEU), 43

Maggio, Sam, 56
Mahmood, Bashiruddin, 32–33
Malashenko, Alexey, 31
Malic, Constantin, 30
Malin, Martin B.
 on danger of complacency, 66
 on global nuclear security framework,
  27
 on HEU research reactors in Russia,
  29
 on securing nuclear stockpiles, 12
 on security situation in India, 34
 on sharing security breach
  information, 54
 on terrorist attacks on Pakistani
  facilities, 33
 on theft of weapons-grade materials
  in Russia, 20
Manhattan (New York City), estimated
 damage from detonation of 10-kiloton
 weapon at Grand Central Station,
 10–11
Medalia, Jonathan, 57–58
millirem, defined, 52
mixed oxide (MOX) fuel, 43
Moldova, 30
MOX Fuel Fabrication Plant (South
 Carolina), 43

National Research Council (of the
 National Academies of Sciences,
 Engineering, and Medicine)
 amount of spent fuel stored
  underwater in US, 23
 on detection methods for homeland
  defense, 61, 62
 recommendations for storage of
  spent fuel, 52
National Security Agency (NSA), 63–65
natural language processing, 65, 66
New York Times (newspaper), 32, 33
North Atlantic Treaty Organization, 18
North Korea, 33, 36–37
nuclear attacks, types of, 9–10, **10**
nuclear bombs
 detonation of, 9–11, **10**
 dismantling of, **42**

materials required, 12
types of, 21
nuclear car washes, 58–61
nuclear facilities
    measures controlling access, 23–24
    oversight of building of, and of waste
        from, 13
    sabotage of, 10, 11
    See also nuclear power plants;
        nuclear waste
nuclear power plants
    cyberattacks on, 36–37
    fuel used in, 20–21, 43, **44**, 44–45
    Fukushima Daiichi in Japan, 11
    global overview of, 22
    percentage of global energy supplied
        by, 52
    plutonium as by-product of uranium
        fuel, 21, 41
    sabotage in Belgium, 34–36
    South Texas Project plant robot test,
        56
    in US, 22
Nuclear Regulatory Commission (NRC,
    in US), 13, 22, 49–50
Nuclear Security Summit, 17–18, 28,
    31
nuclear waste
    consolidation of storage sites, 46–51
    in once-through (open) and closed
        fuel cycles, 14, **14**
    oversight of, 13
    regulation of, in US, 22
    sealing in salt, 47
    storage of, in US
        temporary in Texas, 50
        underwater, 23
        Waste Isolation Pilot Plant, 43–44,
            47, 50
        Yucca Mountain, 22–23, **23**, 47,
            50, 51–52
    transportation of, **49**, 49–51
nuclear weapons
    under control of US in foreign nations,
        18
    measures controlling access, 23–24
    measures controlling use, 24
    nations possessing, 18
    permissive action links, 60
    self-protection, 60

Obama, Barack
    2009 address to UN Security Council,
        17
    Nuclear Security Summit, 17–18
    on plutonium produced by power
        plants, 41
    sanctions against Russia, 28
    storage of nuclear waste, 22
    Yucca Mountain and, 51
once-through (open) cycle
    nuclear waste in, 14, **14**
    requiring, 41

Pakistan
    ability to produce weapons-grade
        plutonium, 32
    closed fuel cycle in power plants,
        21
    security measures described, 19
    security problems in, 32–33
permissive action links, 60
plutonium
    amount stored in US, 40, 45–46, 47
    attempted smuggling or sale of, 24
    ceasing production of, 41–42
    downblending, 42–44
    IAEA definition of significant amount
        of, 60
    importance of, 12
    Indian ability to produce weapons-
        grade, 34
    manufacture of, 13
    in nature, 13
    Pakistani ability to produce weapons-
        grade, 32
    produced in nuclear power plants,
        20–21, 41
    radiation detection equipment and,
        45
    radioisotope fingerprint/signature,
        61–62
    Russian corruption and, 30–31
    unaccounted for, 53
    See also weapons-grade materials
Priest, Dana, 64
Putin, Vladimir, 17, 31

al Qaeda, 9, 31, 33

radiation-detecting wands, **63**

radiation detection equipment
  current, 58
  plutonium and, 45
  possible future, 58–61, **63**
  at Russian borders, 28–29
  at US borders, **25**, 25–26
radiation portal monitors (RPMs), **25**, 25–26
radioactive decay, 12
radioactive materials, 12
radioisotopes, defined, 61
radiological dispersal devices. *See* dirty bombs
repository, defined, 22
research reactors, fuel in, 20, 29
robots, 55–56
Roth, Nickolas
  on danger of complacency, 66
  on global nuclear security framework, 27
  on HEU research reactors in Russia, 29
  on securing nuclear stockpiles, 12
  on security situation in India, 34
  on sharing security breach information, 54
  on terrorist attacks on Pakistani facilities, 33
  on theft of weapons-grade materials in Russia, 20
Russia
  amount agreed to downblend or immobilize, 45
  amount of HEU downblended by, 43
  antiballistic missile treaty with US (as Soviet Union), 18–19
  breakdown of cooperation with US, 28
  government corruption, 30–31, 35
  incursion into Ukraine, 28
  security gaps in, 28–31, **29**, 32
  terrorist threat within, 31
  unaccounted-for plutonium from Soviet Union, 53
  upgraded security measures in, 20

salt, 47
security engineering, 50–51
Seife, Charles, 64
Sharia4Belgium, 35–36

Sheets, Lawrence Scott, 35
Siberian Chemical Combine, 30–31
South Korea, 36–37
Soviet Union
  antiballistic missile treaty with US, 18–19
  unaccounted-for plutonium from, 53
  weapons-grade materials in former members of, 20
  See also Russia
spent fuel. *See* nuclear waste
spies, 62
Starostin, Alexey, 31
Stuxnet computer worm, 36
subatomic, defined, 58
Sunday Morning Herald (Australian newspaper), 48

terrorists
  infiltration of Indian Air Force Base by Pakistani, 34
  number of attacks since 1970, 8–9
  in Pakistan, 32–33
  sabotage of nuclear power plant in Belgium, 34–36
  securing stockpiles against, 12
  seeking nuclear weapons, 9
  tracking, 62–64
thermonuclear bombs, 21
Time (magazine), 9
Tobey, William H.
  on danger of complacency, 66
  on global nuclear security framework, 27
  on HEU research reactors in Russia, 29
  on securing nuclear stockpiles, 12
  on security situation in India, 34
  on sharing security breach information, 54
  on terrorist attacks on Pakistani facilities, 33
  on theft of weapons-grade materials in Russia, 20
Transparency International, 29–30, 33
Treaty on the Limitation of Anti-Ballistic Missile Systems (1972), 18–19
Twitter, 64–65
two-person rule, 24, 54–55, **55**

Ukraine, 28
Union of Concerned Scientists, 40, 43, 45
United Kingdom, 50
United Nations (UN), 16
United States
  Advance Orion spy satellites, 63
  amount of HEU and plutonium agreed to downblend or immobilize, 45
  amount of HEU and plutonium downblended by, 43
  amount of plutonium held by, 40, 45–46, 47
  antiballistic missile treaty with Soviet Union, 18–19
  border control measures, **25**, 25–26, 57–58
  breakdown of cooperation with Russia, 28
  electronic eavesdropping, GPS tracking, and video surveillance in, 64
  global financial assistance for nuclear security reduced or terminated, 28, 32, 34
  Internet activity monitoring in, 64–65
  MOX Fuel Fabrication Plant, 43
  nuclear power plants in, 22
  Nuclear Regulatory Commission, 13, 49–50
  nuclear waste storage
    EPA requirements for, 51
    temporary in Texas, 50
    underwater, 23
    Waste Isolation Pilot Plant, 43–44, 47, 50
    Yucca Mountain, 22–23, **23**, 47, 50, 51–52
  nuclear weapons systems, 37–39, **38**
  radiation detection at borders, **25**, 25–26
  weapons under control of, in foreign nations, 18
uranium
  in nature, 13
  in nuclear fuel cycle, 14, **14**

plutonium as by-product of, in nuclear power plants, 41
used in nuclear power plants, 20–21
See also highly enriched uranium (HEU)
US Department of Energy (DOE), 22, **42**, 45
US Department of Homeland Security, **25**, 25–26, 58, 64
US Environmental Protection Agency (EPA), 51
USS John Warner, **38**

voice recognition software, 65

Washington Post (newspaper), 64
Waste Control Specialists (WCS), 50
Waste Isolation Pilot Plant (WIPP, New Mexico), 43–44, 47, 50
weapons-grade materials
  destruction of, 40
  location of, 19–20
  reducing amount of
    ceasing plutonium production, 41–42
    downblending, 42–44
    immobilization, 44–45
  reduction of number of storage sites of, 46
  See also highly enriched uranium (HEU); plutonium
weapons systems, cyberattacks on, 37–39, **38**
Wier, Anthony, 10
worm, defined, 36

Yanukovych, Viktor, 28
YouTube, 64–65
Yucca Mountain (US), **23**
  about, 22, 47
  environmental impact concerns about, 22–23
  private sector alternative to, 50
  water concerns, 51–52
Yukiya Amano, 22

Zittrain, Jonathan, 57

ABOUT THE AUTHOR

Bradley Steffens is an award-winning poet, playwright, novelist, and author of more than thirty nonfiction books for children and young adults. He is a two-time recipient of the San Diego Book Award for Best Young Adult and Children's Nonfiction: His *Giants* won the 2005 award, and his *J.K. Rowling* claimed the 2007 prize. Steffens also received the Theodor S. Geisel Award for best book by a San Diego County author in 2007.